FOLK-TALES OF HINDUSTAN

FOLK-TALES OF HINDUSTAN

SHAIKH CHILLI

GYAN

Published by

Gyan Publishing House
5, Ansari Road
Daryaganj, New Delhi-110002
Phone: 011-47034999, 9811692060
E-mail: books@gyanbooks.com

Distribution Network
gyanbooks.com
India, USA, Canada, UK, Australia, France

ISBN:978-81-212-8989-4 (PB)
First Published, 1913

2nd Impression 2023

Printed at: Gyan Press, Delhi.

FOLK-TALES OF HINDUSTAN

AUTHOR: SHAIKH CHILLI

PLATE XXXIV.

The *Peris* dance round the dead body of the King of Persia.

FOLK-TALES OF HINDUSTAN

BY

SHAIKH CHILLI

SECOND EDITION

Illustrated by U. Ray & Sons

PANINI OFFICE,
BAHADURGANJ, ALLAHABAD

1913

PRINTED AND PUBLISHED BY ABINASH CHANDRA SARKAR,
AT THE
"BRAHMO MISSION PRESS"
211, Cornwallis Street, CALCUTTA

To

The Hon'ble

Sir James Scorgie Meston, K. C. S. I.,

The Enlightened and Sympathetic

Ruler of the Provinces

where these stories are listened to

by young and old alike

This Book

is respectfully dedicated

with permission

by

his most obedient servant,

The Author.

CONTENTS

—0—

LIST OF ILLUSTRATIONS

PREFACE

These stories originally appeared in their present form in the *Modern Review* with the introduction printed in this book. They are given as narrated by village folk, with slight omissions and alterations to suit the needs of juvenile readers.

Their wide appreciation is the reason why they are now presented to the public in the form of a book. That they appeal even to the taste of foreign readers is clear from the following remarks, which appeared in the *Review of Reviews* for October, 1907 :—

"*The Modern Review* contains, month by month, stories of a type that recall the delightful romances of the 'Arabian Nights.' In the September Number Shaikh Chilli tells the story of Prince Mahbub which vies with the stories of Princess Sheherzadi.

INTRODUCTION

——o——

[Folklore is a comparatively new science. What is now considered as its working definition is that given by Mr. Gomme. His definition of the science is—"the science which treats of the survivals of archaic beliefs and customs in modern ages." His divisions of the materials on which this science is based are: (1) *Traditional Narratives*: (*a*) Folk-tales, (*b*) Hero-tales, (*c*) Ballads and Songs, (*d*) Place Legends; (2) *Traditional Customs*: (*a*) Local Customs, (*b*) Festival Customs, (*c*) Ceremonial Customs, (*d*) Games; (3) *Superstitions* and *Beliefs*: (*a*) Witchcraft, (*b*) Astrology, (*c*) Superstitious Practices and Fancies; (4) *Folkspeech*: (*a*) Popular Sayings, (*b*) Popular Nomenclature, (*c*) Proverbs, (*d*) Jingle Rhymes, Riddles, &c.

The task of the folklorist is to construct the philosophy of primitive man from his still surviving relics. It was not till after the beginning of the Ninetenteh Century that the value of folklore for the elucidation of the social history of mankind became apparent to thinkers, and its systematic study seriously began. The brothers Grimm in Germany were the first to study folk-tales scientifically. It has since been found that the history of a story is often more interesting and more instructive than the history of a campaign. The literature of folklore has already attained vast proportions. The library of folklore and folk-tales actually extends to thousands of volumes. In Europe and America there are many Folklore Societies, and many journals devoted to the Science. So widely popular have folklore studies become in France that a special congress of its students was held at Paris during the great Exposition of 1889. However puerile or absurd a folk-tale may at first appear, it is really a fit subject for scientific investigation and capable of yielding scientific results. We in India, however, have left even the collection of folk-tales to be done by foreigners for the most part, considering these stories to be unworthy the attention of so metaphysical a race as ourselves. But we must, if we want to survive, take our place by the side of the progressive races of the world in all departments of scientific study and research. The writer of the FOLK-TALES OF HINDUSTAN is simply contributing materials for the folklorist. Their study must be left to other hands.

There may be others who may undertake the task of accumulating similar materials in different parts of India. These would-be collectors of folk-tales may take the Grimms' method of editing as their canon : 'Our first aim in collecting these stories has been exactness and truth. We have added nothing of our own, have embellished no incident or feature of the story, but have given its substance just as we ourselves received it. It will, of course, be understood that the mode of telling and carrying out of particular details is principally due to us, but we have striven to retain everything that we knew to be characteristic, that in this respect also we might leave the collection the many-sidedness of nature.'

"The Grimms early found a startling similarity in the

substance of these stories, and it only remained for later workers to discover the same identities when the comparison was extended far beyond the range of Aryan affinities. It was found that certain incidents, plots, and characteristics occurred everywhere—as the ill-treatment of the youngest son or daughter, who is eventually successful, and is often the heir; the substitution of a false bride for the true; the abduction of a bride by a youthful hero, and the pursuit by her giant (or supernatural) father, who is outwitted by cunning; a supernatural husband or wife, who is for some cause obliged to abandon a human mate; forbidden chambers, and the disasters that follow from their being opened; descents into the world of gloom, and the danger of eating there; husband and wife forbidden to see each other or name each other's names; the souls of the dead entering animal forms; and the interchange of kindly offices, as if on equal terms, between men and beasts."—Ed., *M. R.*]

FOLK-TALES OF HINDUSTAN

THE STORY OF THE GREATER FOOL

Two friends were passing through a street when an old woman saluted them both with a *salaam*. The friends began to quarrel as to whom the woman had *salaamed*, and when they could not come to any settlement of the dispute, they resolved to refer the matter to the old woman. So they ran quickly after her crying, "O Mamma, Mamma, wait a moment and resolve our doubt." The woman stopped and asked what the matter was. The friends said, "Mamma, whom did you salute ?" The old woman replied, "I saluted the greater fool of you two." Then each began to claim superiority over the other in folly and stupidity. The woman said, "I cannot decide such a delicate question on your mere assertions ; let me hear your histories and then I will give my award."

One of the friends then related his story in the following words :—

Once upon a time in a hot summer day I was taking a walk in a garden. When oppressed with heat, I laid myself down to sleep by the brink of a well. I was soon lost in deep sleep and when I awoke I found that my turban had fallen into the well and that my shoes had been taken away by some dog or thief. I was very much troubled what to do and knew not how to return home. However, mustering courage, I ran home barefooted and bareheaded, but covering the head with my hands. My maid- servant, seeing me running homewards in this condition, ran weeping to her mistress and informed her, "O *Begam*, some great misfortune has befallen us, as *Mian* is running here barefooted and striking his bare forehead." As soon as the news of my coming reached the family they set up loud wails and lamentation. When I reached home I found all weeping and tearing their hair. I did not know that I was the cause of all this grief. I naturally thought that some great calamity must have befallen our family; so I also without any enquiry sat down amongst them and wept very bitterly. Our cries brought in the neighbours, who also out of sympathy joined in the chorus. After an hour or so of weeping the neighbours asked me, "Friend, who is dead?" I said, "I do not know, ask my family." Upon this my servant said, "Heigh Sir, we wept because we saw you run home in a distracted fashion." When I told my story, all cried out that I was the greatest fool alive.

The other friend then told his story thus:—

I was invited by my father-in-law a few days after my marriage to a feast. My friends advised me, all saying, "Beware how you behave yourself there. It is not good-breeding for a son-in-law to eat or drink much or to show that he is hungry. So be circumspect in your diet." I promised to do as they advised. When I reached the house of my father-in-law, I found great preparations had been made to receive me. Dishes nicely cooked were placed before me, and my mouth watered to taste those delicacies. But true to my promise, I did not eat a single mouthful, and when my mother-in-law pressed me to eat, I excused myself,

Plate I.

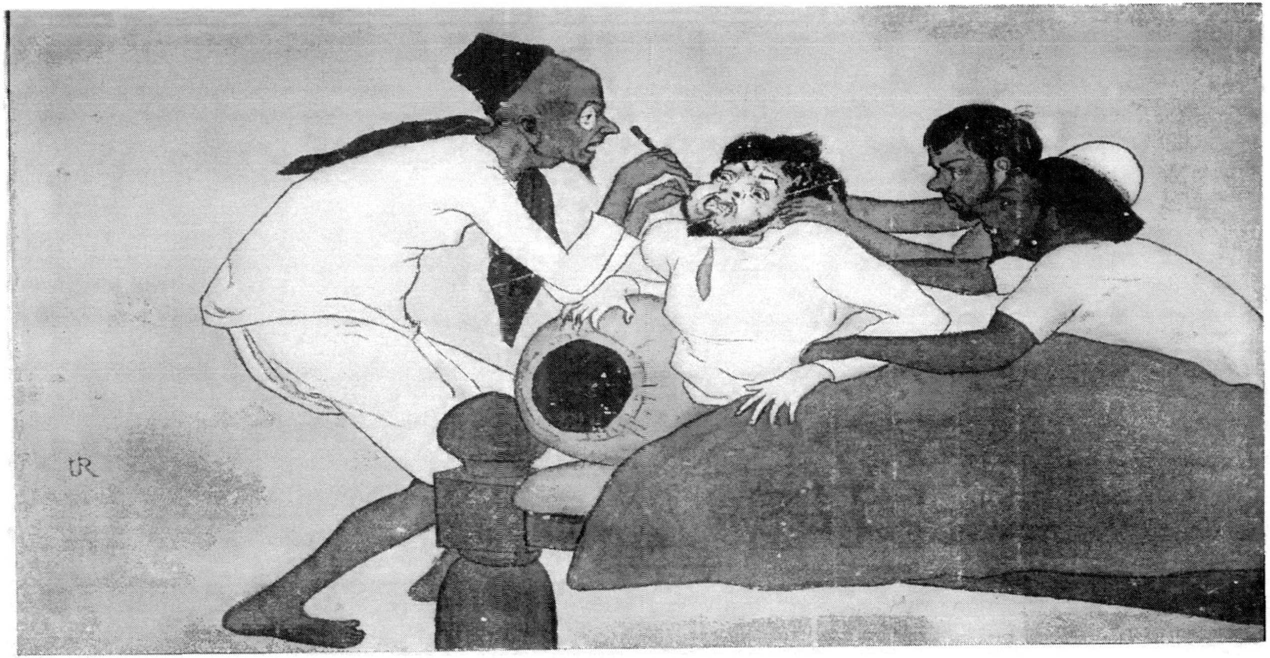

He made a deep incision in my right cheek."

"I have got stomach-ache and indigestion; so kindly excuse me." Thus I fasted all the day, but when it was midnight, my hunger was so great that I would have gnawed my own bones to satisfy it. So I groped my way to the kitchen, to see whether I could find anything there to eat. I searched here and there but without success, till I found some eggs in a corner. I took as many as my hands could hold and ran towards my sleeping room. But unfortunately in my haste I fell down with a loud noise, just at the door of my bedchamber. The sound roused the inmates of the house and they ran to see what was the matter. I quickly entered the room and laid myself on the bed, but found no time to hide the eggs. So in order to escape detection, I thrust them all into my mouth, and, believe me, it was swollen and as big as a melon, and I was almost choked to death. When they came into my room they found my mouth swollen fearfully, and asked what was the matter. I did not reply but kept my mouth more tightly closed; fearing lest by speaking I should show them the eggs within. Seeing that I neither spoke nor answered their queries in any other way, my mother-in-law and others began to cry, saying, "Poor boy, he is dying of starvation. See how big his mouth is, inflamed with cold and hunger. Send for a *hakim* quickly." A physician was at once called in, and he also seeing me silent and my eyes bursting with suffocation pronounced that I was suffering from a most dangerous form of inflammation of the cheek and that a surgical operation must be instantaneously performed to relieve me of it. So taking a sharp knife he made a deep incision in my right cheek, cutting one of the eggs within; and out came the white and the yolk of it through the hole. The physician most triumphantly said, "Behold what an amount of putrid matter was in it." Then he made an incision in the other cheek and the knife this time broke two eggs, and more yolk and albumen came out this time and the physician again cried out, "Behold the *pus.*" I was well-nigh out of my senses with pain and anger, and, spitting out the eggs, cried with great indignation:—"Foolish Doctor, it is no *pus* or putrid matter which you have extracted but the white and yellow of eggs. Are you not the greatest of fools in confounding the two?" I hoped by this timely retort to crush the doctor for ever, for he was a pig-headed, self-opinioned old rascal and gave very bitter pills to his patients and killed more than he cured. But what was my horror when the table was turned on me, and all began to laugh and say, "You are the greater fool of the two."

When the old woman heard these stories, she was also of the same opinion, saying, "Your friend is a great fool, but I congratulate you on being a greater. I saluted *you.*"

THE STORY OF THE SHREW AND THE SHADE

On an old banyan tree, there lived a ghost of a Brahman who had committed suicide in a fit of religious fanaticism. Near the tree there dwelt a family of Brahmans who were specially under the protection of the ghost. The ancient ghost belonged to the family, and always took great care to show his kindness to the old stock in diverse pleasant ways, such as throwing stones, bones, rubbish, dung, night-soil, &c.; making hideous noises, and terrifying the members by frightful appearances. Under such fostering patronage the family soon dwindled away, and nothing flourished with them, and one by one all of them died and joined the majority, leaving none to offer them water and cake except a half-crazed fellow whose existence the ghost thought it beneath his dignity to recognise. But though he was an idiot, birth, marriage and death come to all, as the Shastras say; and so all the neighbours held a *Panchayet* to consult about the marriage of the idiot. After due deliberation they unanimously agreed:—1st, that the idiot should be married, otherwise it would be a standing reproach to the whole community, and a disgrace to the neighbourhood; 2ndly, that he should be married to the daughter of a neighbour, a girl who had reached the most extraordinary age of fourteen years without being married, for she was a curst shrew and no one would marry her. So after all married he was, for the *Panchayet* had ruled it, and the Shastras declare that a man without a spouse is but the half of himself, and a house without a wife is a *masan* (a place of execution). Though the neighbours had done their duty very conscientiously by bringing about the marriage, they very wisely left them to their resources to manage for their livelihood. The poor fellow of an idiot used to get his bread by begging, and could hardly support himself, and a wife was now to him an additional burden. The first thing which the shrew did when she came to his house was to give him a round box in his ear and order him out of the house to seek for a livelihood. The poor fellow went out and begged from door to door all the day, but no one would now give him even his usual dole of pittance; for the people were enraged with him, as he had not given the *Biradari* the customary marriage feast. He went through the town all the day, and returned in the evening, weary and disappointed. No sooner did the shrew see him, than she cried out, "Hast thou returned, thou lazy disgrace of Brahmans? What wast thou doing so long and what hast thou brought for me?" With this she rushed upon him, searched him and when she found that he had brought nothing, her rage knew no bounds. She tore away his turban, and taking it up threw it on the banyan tree, and then taking an old rotten broomstick thrashed him soundly till he rushed out of the house howling with rage and pain. But the anger of the vixen was not yet pacified; so with the stick in her hand she rushed towards the banyan tree and began to strike it furiously, directing her blows towards the turban, which was out of her reach. The shower of blows accompained by the more formidable volley of abuses frightened even the

Plate II.

"Thrashed him soundly till he rushed out of the house howling."

ancient ghost, and he also took to his heels, leaving the tree on which he had dwelt for so many centuries.

In the meantime the idiot had also run out of the city, and had resolved not to return to his home, so long as the shrew was alive. Now as he was walking sad and melancholy, he was espied by the ghost, who was riding on a whirlwind and was also running away from the tyranny of the shrew. Misery makes common bed-fellows of us all, and the great spirit who had so long disdained to cast his eyes upon the idiot, now accosted him spontaneously: "Ram, Ram, brother, do you not recognise me? I am the ghost who was your neighbour so long. I, too, am a victim of that shrew, your wife; and so henceforth will look upon you as my brother, as we will seek out our fortune together. Promise that you will never return to her." The idiot was but too glad to get this timely help, and gave the required promise most willingly.

Thus they went on and on, till they reached a large city. Before entering it, the ghost said to the idiot:—"Brother, hear what I tell you and if you follow my advice your fortune is made. In this city there are two very beautiful girls, the daughter of the vazir, and the daughter of the Sultan. I will go and possess the daughter of the vazir and her father will employ every sort of remedy without effect. You must also walk daily through the streets in the garb of a holy *faqir*, and when the vazir will come to you and ask you to cure his daughter, make any terms you think proper for your trouble. As soon as I shall see you, I will leave her. Then I will go and attack the daughter of the Sultan, but mind you never go there, for I love her and will never leave her. If you venture to go there, I will break your neck." Saying this the ghost vanished, and the idiot entered the city alone and put up in an obscure lodging house.

The next day, the city was deeply agitated with the news that the beautiful daughter of the vazir was dangerously ill. Surgeons and physicians, *hakims* and *baids*, saw her and pronounced her case hopeless. The poor father was distracted with grief at the idea of losing his only child, and he offered half his wealth to anybody who would cure her. The idiot in the meantime, having besmeared himself well with ashes and mud, began to parade through the streets, occasionally crying out in strange, weird tones:—"*Bhum, Bhum, Bho ; Bom Bhola Nath.*" The people seeing him in this attire, and struck by his speech and demeanour, took him to be a very holy saint and reported him to the vazir. At once the latter came with all his train, and prostrating himself before the idiot, entreated him to cure his daughter. The idiot after much show of reluctance was prevailed upon to go to the house of the vazir. The girl was brought before him, with her hair dishevelled and glaring eyes, and howling and cursing and tearing her clothes. When he saw her, he cried out in a commanding tone:

> "*Bhut, pret, pisach, dana,*
> *Chhoo mantar, sab nikal jana,*
> *Mano, mano, Shib ka kahna* ;" *i. e.*,
> "Sprite and ghost, goblin and fay,
> Hear the charm and fly away,
> Obey, obey ; thus Shiva doth say."

He thundered forth many more meaningless *mantras* till the ghost cried out, as if in mortal terror:—"I go, O Lord, I go, I go." The idiot then asked the *bhut*, according to orthodox fashion, to give some sign that he had left the girl. The sprite said, "You will know for certain that I have left this girl as soon as you see yonder tree uprooted. That is the sign which I give." Saying this the ghost left the girl, and uprooted the tree in his passage. This news was soon circulated throughout the city, and the idiot was now an object of wonder and adoration for the whole town. The vazir also fulfilled his promise and gave him half of his wealth; and thus he began to live happily.

After a few weeks the *bhut* took possession of the princess; and as the fame of the idiot had reached even the king, royal emissaries were sent to fetch him. But the idiot would not come; he remembered what the ghost had threatened. Greatly was he tempted with offers of riches, honours and position, but he did not waver. At last the Sultan was enraged against him; and sent his executioners with orders to strike off his head if he would not come. After this the poor fellow could no longer refuse to go. He accompanied the royal officer to the palace, thinking and racking his poor brain about some means of saving his neck from the anger of the ghost. No sooner did the ghost see his quondam protege than he cried out in great rage, "Foolish idiot, why hast thou broken thy compact, and ventured into my presence? Thy days are numbered, and the gates of hell are open for thee. Behold, I break thy neck." Then the idiot said, "Brother *bhut*, I have not come to torment you but to tell you a terrible piece of news.

I must not utter it in public, but must whisper it into your ears." Saying this, he approached the princess and said in a very low whisper, "Alas! brother *bhut*, my protector, guardian and master, under the shadow of whose ægis, generations after generations of my family had flourished and thrived, and through whose kindness and affection I have risen to this affluence; alas, alas, we must leave this city soon; for SHE has come,—the dreaded shrew, even now she is coming towards the palace and will be here in a few minutes." And after this the idiot made a great show of weeping. No sooner did the ghost hear this than he screamed out, "I go, I go, SHE has come even here, I go, I go. Break open the doors, pull down the walls. SHE has come, I go, I go." And there was great shaking of the doors and falling of walls and the ghost departed in a hurry far far away and for ever. The idiot was after this made the son-in-law of the Sultan and succeeded to the kingdom on the death of the latter.

THE STORY OF THE JAT AND THE BANIA

In a certain village there lived a Bania, who kept a shop of rice, wheat, salt, oil, &c., and supplied all the small wants of its little community. One day, while on the way to the neighbouring town to make purchases for his shop, he met a poor Jat (one of a caste of cultivators), who was also going to the town to pay his monthly instalment of debt to the Mahajan (banker). It was a debt incurred by his great-grandfather to celebrate the obsequies of *his* great-grandfather. The debt which in the beginning was but a hundred rupees, had grown ten-fold during half a century with interest and compound interest. The poor fellow was cogitating as to how to save his ancestral lands from the clutches of the money-lender, when he was accosted by the Bania in the following words: "Well met, Chowdhri. I see you are going to your inexorable Mahajan to pay your instalment. Can nothing be done to save your lands?" The poor Jat said, "Ah Shahjee! it is a sad tale, as you know. My great-grandfather borrowed a hundred rupees; and the amount has swollen to one thousand rupees. How can my few *bighas* of land pay up such a large sum?" "Do not grieve, Bhai Chowdhri; what is written on one's forehead must happen. So instead of bewailing your lot let us beguile the tedium of this long journey by telling stories." "Well suggested, Shahjee! I perfectly agree; there is no use weeping over that which is written in our *kismat*. So let us beguile the irksomeness of the journey by telling stories. But let this be the condition that howsoever untrue or absurd the story may be, neither of us must call it untrue or even fictitious. He who does so must pay to the other a thousand rupees." "Agreed," said the Bania. "Let me begin my tale," he added, and proceeded thus :—

"You know my great-grandfather was the greatest man among the Banias, and was exceedingly rich."

"True, O Shahjee, true!" said the Jat.

"Now this great ancestor of mine once equipped forty ships and sailed to China and trafficked there in rich jewels and precious stones."

"True, O Shahjee, true!" said the Jat.

"Well, when he had remained there long enough to amass a large fortune, he returned home, bringing with him many curiosities from that country. Among them there was a speaking statue of pure gold of such cunning workmanship that it could answer all questions put to it."

"True, O Shahjee, true!" said the Jat.

"When my ancestor returned home, many came to have their fortune told by that wonderful statue and went away satisfied with its replies. One day your great-grandfather came to my ancestor to ask some questions of the speaking statue. He asked :—'What caste of men is the wisest of all?' The statue replied, 'The Bania.' He next asked, 'What caste is the most foolish on earth?' The reply was, 'The Jat.' The last question your great-grandfather asked was, 'Who will be the greatest blockhead in my family?' The statue replied, 'Chowdhri *Lahri Singh*.'" (That was the name of our Jat hero.)

"True, O Shahjee, true!" said the Jat, though the covert hit of the Bania went to his heart; and he inwardly vowed to repay the Bania in his own coin, and in such measure that he would rue it to the end of his days.

"Well, then," went on the Bania, "the fame of the statue spread far and wide, and reached the king, who summoning my great-grandfather, made him his Prime Minister, in exchange for the statue."

"True, O Shahjee, true!" said the Jat.

"My great-grandfather remained long the trusted and faithful counseller of the Raja, and when he died, my grandfather succeeded to the post. He lived in great affluence, but, not paying as much attention to his work as the Raja wished, he soon incurred the displeasure of the king and was ordered to be trampled to death by an elephant. He was placed before a mad elephant, but as soon as the brute saw him, he became calm, and, bowing down before my ancestor, lifted him with his trunk upon his back."

"True, O Shahjee, true!" said the Jat.

"Well, then, when the king saw that the mad elephant would not kill my grandfather, he got pacified, and re-instated him in his favour and conferred great honours upon him. On the death of my grandfather, my father became Prime Minister, but, being of an enterprising turn of mind, he relinquished his situation and went on travel. In his tour round the world he saw many wonders, as for instance, men with one leg who hung head downwards from the branches of trees, one-eyed men, giants, &c. One day my father perceived a mosquito, hovering near his ear to bite him. My father was sorely dismayed, not knowing what to do, as you know we, Banias, are forbidden to kill any living creature."

"True, O Shahjee, true!" said the Jat.

"So then, in great distress, my father fell on his knees and implored the mercy of the insect. On being thus entreated the mosquito said, 'Most noble Shahjee! You are the greatest man I have seen. I will do you a great service.' Saying this the mosquito opened its mouth, and my father saw within it a large palace of burning gold, with many windows, eaves, gates &c., and at one of the windows the most beautiful female figure he had ever seen. On the door of the palace he saw a peasant about to attack the princess. My father, who was famous for his spirit of chivalry, at once jumped into the mouth of the mosquito and entered its stomach. It was all dark and he found himself groping in the belly of the insect."

"True, O Shahjee, true!" said the Jat.

"After some time, the darkness melted away and my father again saw the palace, the princess, and the peasant. My father, being a very courageous man, fell upon the peasant, who was no other than your father. They fought for a year in the stomach of the mosquito; after which period your father acknowledged himself vanquished and gave up all claims to the princess. So my father married the princess and lived in that palace, and I was born there. Your father remained in the service of my father as door-keeper and used to sit the whole day and night at the door keeping watch. When I was fifteen years old, a heavy rain of boiling water fell upon our palace, which melting away threw us into a burning sea. After much trouble we reached the shore, and we four, *viz.*, my father, your father, the princess and myself, jumped at once from the sea upon

Plate III.

"They fought for a year in the stomach of the mosquito."

the shore. When lo! we found ourselves in a kitchen, and the cook looking terror-stricken at our appearance! After some minutes, when she had been assured that we were men and not ghosts, she said, 'You are nice fellows to spoil my broth. What business had you to enter that pot of boiling water in which I was cooking my fish and frighten me thus?" We all apologised to her and said, 'If we were in that pot, it was through ignorance. For it is fifteen years since we have been living in a palace within the belly of a mosquito.' 'Ah! I remember,' said the cook, 'just fifteen minutes ago I saw a mosquito which bit me on my arm. Here is the wound which the wretch inflicted. I fear you must have been injected into my arm by the insect: for I felt extraordinary pain. I squeezed out the poison, and saw a black drop as large as this mustard seed, and it happened to fall into the boiling water, and I never imagined that you were in it.' My father replied, 'Bibiji, this seems to be the most satisfactory explanation of how we came into the pot. Our fifteen years must have been your fifteen minutes.' In fact, I was but fifteen minutes old, though in stature and strength I was like a boy of fifteen years. We found to our surprise that we had been only fifteen minutes in the belly of the insect, though in that short space of time I was born, and grown so big, and my father and thy father had grown older by fifteen years. Though I look like a man of five and twenty or thereabouts, I am in reality a child of ten years, my extraordinary growth being the result of my fifteen minutes' residence in the burning belly of the mosquito."

"True, O Shahjee, true!" said the Jat.

"When we came out we found that we had come to another country, that, in fact, we were in this village. So my father, who was Prime Minister before now, took to shop-keeping and I to helping him. The princess, my mother, died the other day as you know. This is my story."

"True, O Shahjee, true!" said the Jat.

"Your story is very true. My story, though not less true, is, I fear, not so wonderful. But it is perfectly true, yea, every word of it. Now hear it with attention :—

"My great-grandfather was the most well-to-do Jat in the whole village. His distinguished appearance, noble demeanour and profound wisdom extorted praise from all who came in contact with him. He was universally respected in the community, and being the headman of the village, his voice was ever raised in defence of the weak. In the *Chowpal* and village meetings the foremost seat was always given to him, and the *hooka* invariably first offered to him. He was loved by all for his many good qualities; whenever any poor fellow was in distress, he would help him by every means in his power; he would gladly lend his oxen to others to plough their fields; he would send his own men to reap the harvest for others when they were short of hands; and everybody was welcome to a share in the produce of his fields and dairy. He settled all the disputes of the community; and there was none who questioned his authority. In fact, his mandates had greater force than the edicts of the Emperor or the decrees of the *Kazi*. He was a terror to the wicked, for, being of great physical strength, greater than that of Rustam or

Plate IV.

" My ancestor went about in search of rain."

Bhim Sen, none dared incur his displeasure by any transgression of the human or divine law."

"True, O Chowdhri, true," said the Bania.

"Well, once upon a time there was a great famine in our village. No rain fell on the land, the rivers and wells dried up and the trees withered away. The cattle starved for want of fodder, and birds and beasts died on all sides in thousands. When my great-grandfather saw that the stores of the last year were exhausted, and the people would soon die of hunger if prompt steps were not taken to remedy the evil, he called together all the Jats and addressed them thus :—'Brother Jats, surely the god Indra has become angry with us, or he would not have withheld rain. I see clearly that we must all soon die of hunger, if measures be not taken to meet the calamity. If you hear my advice, I will try to supply you with food during the entire season of scarcity. I only want that you should all give up your fields to me for six months so that I may make them fruitful.' 'Agreed,' cried unanimously all the Jats. Well then, my great ancestor at once girded up his loins, and by one strong pull lifted up the whole village of a thousand bighas of land and placed it on his head."

"True, O Chowdhri, true!" said the Bania, smiling inwardly at this tissue of preposterous nonsense.

"Well, then, my ancestor, carrying the whole village on his head, went about in search of rain. Wherever it rained there he went with the whole village on his head, and collected all the rain water on the fields and in the reservoirs thereon. Having thus watered the fields he told the Jats to plough up the land and sow the seed. Thus for full six months my great-grandfather went from one country to another, after the clouds and the rains and accumulated all the rainfall of the season in his village. In the meantime his Jats ploughed and sowed, and the crops had never been so splendid. The wheat and the maize stalks being so copiously watered, rose up to such a height that they touched the sky."

"True, O Chowdhri, true!" said the Bania.

"When my ancestor had accomplished his tour round the world with the village and its inhabitants upon his head, he returned to his country and placed the village where it had formerly stood. My great-grandfather reaped a plentiful harvest that year, and the whole village now belonged to him. The growth of the maize and the wheat was prodigious; every grain of corn was as big as your head."

"True, O Chowdhri, true!" said the Bania.

"Well, when all the grain was collected, the produce proved so abundant that there was not room enough to store it in. People from all parts of the country and from distant lands hearing of our wonderful harvest, came to purchase the grain, and great was the profit which my ancestor made by the sales. Thousands and tens of thousands of rupees did my ancestor distribute among the needy; to many he gave the corn *gratis*; from those who could well afford to pay he took but a fair price."

By the time the story of the Jat had reached this point they entered the town, and the Jat went on with his tale as follows :—

"At that time your great-grandfather was a very poor

man, and my ancestor out of pity employed him as a menial servant to weigh out the grain to the customers."

"True, O Chowdhri, true!" said the Bania.

"Your ancestor was employed all day and night in weighing the corn, and was very pitiable to see, and being a blockhead, often made mistakes in counting up the weights of grain he sold; for which he often got good thrashings from my ancestor."

"True, O Chowdhri, true!" said the Bania.

By this time they had entered the shop of the Mahajan (money-lender) to whom the Jat was indebted. They found the banker at his post, and the travellers bidding him "*Ram Ram*," sat down on the floor. But the Jat, without speaking to the banker, went on with his history:—"Well, Shahjee, when my great-grandfather had sold off all the harvest, your great-grandfather's occupation being gone, he was discharged. He then, before going away, asked a loan of my ancestor of one hundred rupees, which the latter generously gave."

"True, O Chowdhri, true!" said the Bania.

"Very good," said the Jat raising his voice, so that the banker might also hear, "Your ancestor did not repay that debt."

"True, O Chowdhri, true!" said the Bania.

"Neither did your grandfather, nor your father pay off that debt, nor have you paid it up to this time."

"True, O Chowdhri, true!" said the Bania.

"Now that sum of one hundred rupees with interest and compound interest at the usual rate makes up exactly one thsusand rupees, which sum you owe me," said the Jat.

"True, O Chowdhri, true!" said the Bania.

"So, as you have admitted the debt before my Mahajan, I request you to pay the amount to him so that I may have my lands released."

This came like a thunder-bolt on the Bania. He had admitted the debt before a third party. He was between the two horns of a dilemma. If he said that it was merely a story and altogether false, he must pay according to the terms of their bet; if he said it was true, he must pay the sum according to his own admission. So, *nolens volens*, he paid up the heavy forfeit and rued his folly for the remainder of his life.

THE STORY OF JANJAL NAGARI

Janjal Nagari was a flourishing town in the province of Andhera-khata—the Land of Darkness. The people of that place were very learned and were reputed for their extraordinary wisdom. There was not a child among them who did not know all about the earth and the movements of the stars and other heavenly bodies. Sextants, globes and astrolabes were the plaything of these infants. The men were very fond of the study of law and metaphysical hair-splitting. No stranger ever visited the town but came out a wiser though a poorer man. Many were seen to enter it who never returned. A rumour had of long been current among the neighbouring towns that the inhabitants of Janjal Nagari were sorcerers, and kept unwary travellers metamorphosed into goats, sheep or other lower animals. Of course, there was no truth in this, and the rumour had its origin in the great learning of the people. In fact, the inhabitants, though very argumentative and contentious, were but a lot of simple creatures, who were totally inexperienced in the practical concerns of life. Their terrible repute had kept them isolated, and they had little occasion for interchanging thoughts with other people.

Once a rich merchant entered the city to make some purchases. He went to the public square, which was the place where every sort of commodity was sold. When he reached it he saw a person crying aloud :—"Three thousand rupees for three good sayings. My name is Hushiar Khan.

I sell proverbs, maxims, words, and advice." The merchant wondered very much in his mind at this strange advertisement, thinking what could be the three sayings for which such a high price was demanded. After a good deal of hesitation, he made up his mind to purchase them. So going up to Hushiar Khan, he offered three purses full of gold, each containing one thousand rupees, and said:—"Sir, here is the money: kindly sell me the sayings." Hushiar Khan took up the purses, counted the money, and then taking the merchant apart, whispered these words in his ears:—"Trust no cook, trust no friend, trust in God." The merchant thought that he had paid too much for the whistle; and his countenance rather betrayed his inward feelings, for he was disappointed. Seeing this, Hushiar Khan said:—"Friend merchant, my object is not to cheat or deceive men. You will understand the truth of these sayings in your own life, and then you will thank me. However, that you may not think that I have overreached you, I give you these seven seeds of mango, orange, guava, apple, melon, pomegranate and grape, which, as soon as you sow them, will grow into big trees in a minute and bear ripe fruits, and then you have only to say vanish and the trees will vanish and you will get back the seeds." The merchant, whose name was Kam-Aql (Little Intellect), was very glad to get such wonderful seeds, and thought himself amply repaid.

When he returned home, the first thing he did was to go to his cook and show him the wonderful seeds. He planted them on a plot of ground before his house, and at once they shot forth into large trees and brought forth

Plate V.

" His countenance rather betrayed his inward feelings."

fruits, and the merchant and his cook ate of them plentifully. and distributed them among his friends, and then he said:—"Vanish," and the trees all vanished, and he got back the seeds. Now the cook was a man of bad character, and dealt in stolen goods with another merchant called Kam-Ikhlaq (Little Morality), who was also a bosom friend of Kam-Aql. The cook of the latter one day finding an opportunity when he was out, called in his partner and said to him :—"Friend, what shall we do now? Since my master brought back those seeds he has left off all idea of going out on travels, and is never absent from home. We cannot enrich ourselves so long as he remains here; you know it was with much difficulty that I had persuaded him to go to Janjal Nagari. I had thought and hoped that he would be metamorphosed there; but unfortunately he has returned again to mar our happiness; moreover he has grown suspicious and watches me strictly. I wish to rid myself of him. Will you help me?" The latter promised to do as he directed, and then he unfolded his plans to him and he approved of them heartily.

When Kam-Aql returned home he found that his friend Kam-Ikhlaq was waiting for him, and very glad was the simple merchant to see his treacherous friend. They sat together, and after the dinner was over, Kam-Ikhlaq suddenly exclaimed, as if the idea had just flashed over his mind:—"Friend, is it true what people say about your wonderful seeds? Do they really grow in a minute? Though some time ago you sent me the fruits, yet I could not believe that they were the products of those seeds. It is so very unnatural." The simple-minded merchant, who had as strong a faith in his seeds as in his senses, replied sharply :—"What, do you think that I have circulated a fib or a falsehood?" The friend replied calmly : "I do not doubt your veracity, but your seeds are so very extraordinary. I cannot bring myself to believe in the existence of such things. Well, if your seeds do grow before my eyes, I promise to give you anything from my house on which you may place your hand and lay hold of, but if you do not succeed, promise that you will give that on which I may first place my hand in your house." "Agreed," cried Kam-Aql, and rushed into the house and said :—"Cook, give me the seeds which I brought from Janjal Nagari, to show its wonderful virtues to my friend Kam-Ikhlaq." The cook gave him the seeds, and he came out with them and sowed them within sight of his friend. What was his surprise and terror when he saw that no trees grew out of them! He then took them out of the ground and carefully examined them, and muttered aside :— "Cursed be thou treacherous man; thou hast boiled these seeds. True are the words of Hushiar Khan, when he said: 'Trust no cook.'" Then addressing his friend Kam-Ikhlaq, he said :—"Look here, friend; these seeds are boiled. I have lost my bet, but it is through no fault of mine. Will you waive your claim?" Then the friend tauntingly replied :—"Ah, I knew that it would come to this. How can there be such seeds? Now I am not to be so easily deceived. Come now, fulfil your promise or I hand you over to justice; do not prattle with me." Then poor Kam-Aql's eyes were opened, and he found that it was all a conspiracy of his friend and his cook, who were both false and faithless. He then implored for fifteen days of grace after which he would fulfil his promise. Kam-Ikhlaq was at first loth to grant this indulgence, but at last after much entreaty and prayers granted the request.

Kam-Aql at once went into a mosque and began to pray, saying:—"Lord, I trusted to a cook, and I found him false, I trusted to a friend, and I found him faithless. I now trust in Thee. So help Thou me." He prayed there for seven days and seven nights, when he heard a voice which said:—"Go to Janjal Nagari, and search out Hushiar Khan; he will help thee out of this difficulty." He at once set out for that city on a horse, upon which he placed his bag of money and precious stones, and reached that city when it was about noon. When he saw the walls of the town, he jumped down from his horse and began to walk through the crowded streets, leading the animal by the rein.

As he was passing through a bazar a butcher met him, who laying his hands on the animal, asked:—" Traveller, what price will you take for this?" Kam-Aql, naturally thinking that the butcher had asked the price of the horse, said:—"Friend, I will sell it for four hundred rupees."

Now this was an exorbitant price for the horse, which was but a sorry jade, but what was his surprise when the butcher counted him out the sum demanded, and taking hold of the rein began to lead it off homeward. Kam-Aql cried out:—"Stay, butcher, stay, let me take away my bag of gold and precious stones, which is hanging by the saddle of the horse." On this the butcher replied:—"Friend, what do you say? Did you not sell me the whole for four hundred rupees? Did you then make any exceptions in favour of your bag or saddle or rein or stirrup?: Am I not justified in taking the animal with everything on it?" said he appealing to the passers-by. And they all decided in favour of the butcher, and he led away the animal and the bag in triumph.

Kam-Aql went forward, very much grieving in his mind at being thus suddenly reduced to poverty in such a strange and ill-reputed city. Complaining against his stars and the evil hour in which he started from home, he began to search out the house of Hushiar Khan. In a street he saw some boys playing. So going up to them he asked the way to Hushiar Khan's house. The boys said:—"What will you give us for showing you the house?" "Why, I will give you the largest lumps of sweetmeats that you ever had," said Kam-Aql. The boys then sat down on the ground; one little urchin took out a sextant, another a compass, and the third one a map of the world. Then observing the position of the sun and the direction of the winds, they made nice calculations, in which the words sines and cosines, latitudes and longitudes fell often upon his ears, and confounded him more and more. After an hour the boys exclaimed:—"We have found it, we have found it." Then they conducted the merchant to the house of Hushiar, cheering and hurrahing all the way. We need not say that the merchant was greatly impressed with the learning and intelligence of these little fellows, but the fact was the boys already knew the house of Hushiar Khan, in fact they were his sons and nephews, and they made this show of learning only to impose upon the stranger. When he reached

Plate VI.

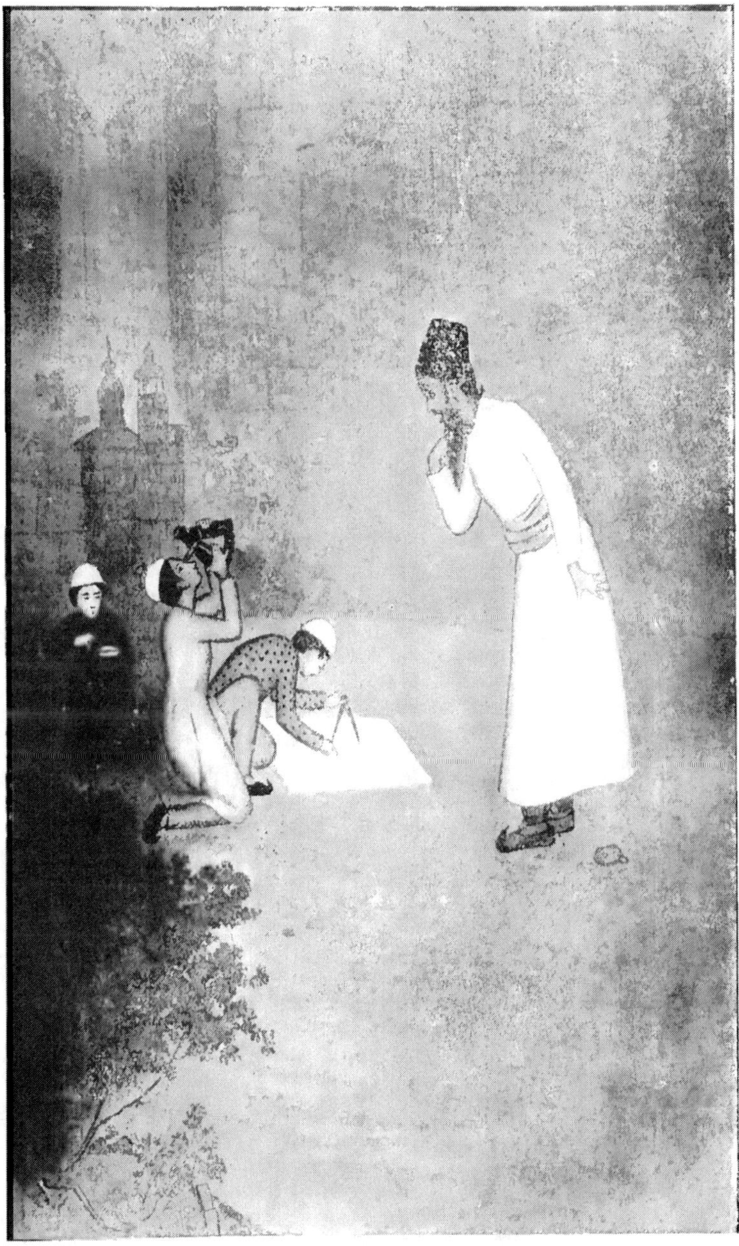

" They made nice calculations."

the house, the boys demanded their reward, and the merchant purchasing a rupee's worth of sweetmeats, presented it to them. The boys would not take it, but said :—"Sir, you promised to give us the *largest lumps*, we will have nothing but the *largest lumps*." The merchant then doubled the quantity, but still they were not satisfied ; he then rose higher, till he gave them fifty rupees' worth of sweetmeats, but still they cried out :—"We will take nothing but the *largest lumps*, we will take nothing but the *largest lumps*, give us the *largest lumps*, we won't take seers, maunds, or tons, but the *largest lumps*." The poor fellow was embarrassed by the obstinacy of the boys and the absurdity of their demand, which was however true according to the letter of his promise, though not its spirit.

In the meantime when the boys were wrangling about the '*largest lumps*' Hushiar Khan came there, and recognising the merchant cordially welcomed him to his home. Then learning the cause of the dispute, he turned towards the boys and said :—"Wait, little gentlemen, for a moment and I will settle matters." He then brought a rupee's worth of sweetmeats, and divided it into as many unequal shares as there were boys, and placing the whole before them, said—"Boys, what do you call these separate heaps of sweetmeats ?" All answered :—"Why, everybody knows it ; they are called lumps." "Well then," said Hushiar Khan, calling out the foremost of them, "take out the largest of these. Now, you have got the largest lump, have you not ?" "Yes," said the boy. Then calling out another, he told him to take up the largest of the remaining lumps, and when he had picked up what appeared to him the largest, he said :—"Now, have you not got the largest lump ?" "Yes, Sir," answered the boy, "I have also got the largest." Similarly every one of the other boys selected from the remainder successively and declared that he had got the largest lump. When they had taken up every one his share, Hushiar Khan addressed them in the following words :—"Friends, as now all of you have got the largest lump, I hope you are satisfied. Now go to school." The boys ran to school, every one congratulating himself on his having got the largest lump, and were never afterwards disabused of their folly and mistake in refusing fifty rupees and contenting themselves with five pice worth of things, till they got a sound caning from their teacher for their folly.

Then Hushiar Khan asked Kam-Aql what business had brought him so far, and learning the whole story, said:—"Friend, do not be cast down, we will soon manage it all, rest now for the night." When it was morn, Hushiar went out to the shop of the butcher and asked :—"Friend, what will you take for all the *sirees* (meaning heads of the slaughtered animals, as well as human heads) that you have got ?" The butcher, who had at that time a hundred heads in his stock, asked a hundred rupees for them all. Hushiar Khan paid him the money, and asked him to bring them out. Then the butcher brought all the *sirees* which he had and gave them to him, and taking up the money was going away, when Hushiar exclaimed :—"Tarry friend, do not play me false. Have you given me all the heads in your house ? I see some sheep and cattle tied up in that shed. Bring their heads too." The butcher *nolens volens* slaughtered them too and gave the heads to him. But Hushiar Khan was not yet satisfied, and said :—"Friend, I saw just now some one peep out of that window. I think she is your daughter, and heard an infant crying, so you have got another child, and I doubt not that you have got a wife too. So bring the heads of these three also, for they have also heads and all heads have been sold to me." The butcher found himself in a fix and falling on his knees asked his mercy and indulgence. Hushiar Khan then thundered out :—"Rascal, you deserve no consideration. But I pardon you this time ; go bring out the horse which you took from my friend yesterday, together with the bag of gold and precious stones, and a thousand rupees as fine for your misconduct." The butcher complied and congratulated himself on his escape.

Hushiar Khan then came home and returning his property to the merchant, said :—"Friend, tarry here for three days, after which we will go to your city and see what can be done. But beware how you conduct yourself in this place. For though the people are not the sorcerers they have been described to be by their enemies, yet they are a headstrong, hair-splitting race of beings. Beware of them." Kam-Aql promised to abide by his advice.

The next day, the merchant had an occasion to buy a pair of shoes, as his old one was no longer fit to be worn. He went to a shoe-maker and said : "Sir, give me a pair of shoes. We shall not have to haggle about the price. I will make you happy (*main tumko khush kar dunga*) ;" meaning, of course, that he would pay a fair and reasonable price. The shoe-maker showed many samples, and the merchant selected the one that best fitted him and offered to pay four rupees, which was the ordinary price of such shoes in his country. But the fellow refused even to touch the money, and the merchant went on offering rupee after rupee till he had paid about fifty rupees. But the shoe-maker would not agree but went on saying :—"Sir, you promised to make me happy, and I ask nothing but to be made happy. I will not accept millions were you to give me so much. I ask nothing but to be made happy." The merchant saw that here was another dilemma, and thought of consulting his friend about it; and, therefore, said :—"Friend, wait till to-morrow, let me consult my friend, and I will fulfil my promise." So returning home Kam-Aql related his adventure to Hushiar, and asked him what to do. The friend said :—"Ah ! Kam-Aql, here is another sign of the wisdom of our people. If they are anything, they are true to their words, and know the value of words. When will you learn to speak simply and rationally ? When will you leave off all similes, metaphors, and what do you call those redundancies, the flowers of speech ? Our people are intensely practical and do not understand your loose mode of transacting business. Weigh well the words you use in your intercourse with them. As regards this little job, you will see how I finish it to-night." When it was about mid-night, Hushiar Khan and his friend took two big *lathis* (sticks) and going up to the shoe-maker's house, began to hammer the door and call aloud :—"Shoe-maker, shoe-maker, are you awake, shoe-maker, are you awake ?" The shoe-maker dreaming that some robbers had come to attack him, jumped out of bed and cried, "who are there ?"

Hushiar Khan replied in a gruff voice :—"We are officers of the king, and have come to inform you that a son and heir-apparent is just born to His Majesty. So get up and make rejoicings, if you are a loyal subject." The shoe-maker hearing the news and in order to please the officers, so that they should make a good report about him, came running down and saying :—"Tarry, gentlemen, tarry, take some refreshments ; you do not know how happy you have made me." "Have we made you happy ?" asked Hushiar Khan. "Undoubtedly," answered the unsuspicious artisan. "Have I made you happy ?" asked Kam-Aql. "Certainly gentlemen you have ; may I take my oath?" said the maker of shoes. Then the friends laughing out said :—"Now friend have you recognized us ? We are not the king's officers. Are we not more than quits ? You said twice that you were happy. Now keep one happiness for yourself, and pay two hundred rupees as the price of the other happiness which we have given you. Certainly you must not enjoy double such mental felicity without paying for it.". The poor artisan was caught in his own snare, and paid the sum demanded without much ado. The two friends shared the profits amongst themselves and returned home in high spirits, chuckling in their minds over the happy issue of their adventure.

The next day Kam-Aql went out to take a walk in the city, inwardly vowing not to have anything to do with its troublesome people, but only to enjoy its fair sights and good buildings. So wandering on he came to a large square, where there was a great gathering, and in the midst of which was a very beautiful woman. She was crying out in a very sweet but loud voice :—"Ten thousand rupees for a summersault in the middle of this square, and in such a public place." Now, cutting a summersault was considered the greatest indelicacy and indecency of which a woman could be guilty; it was an offence which made her liable to be stoned to death, by the laws of the land of which Kam-Aql was the native; and it was held equally indecorous in Janjal Nagari also. Therefore, the first idea of the merchant was that the woman was joking, but when he saw that she was in earnest, he thought 'very well let me test how far the impudence of this female can go, though it may cost me ten thousand rupees.' Then he spoke aloud; "Well, perform the summersault, and I will pay you ten thousand rupees." The woman at once stood on her head, and cut a clean summersault, to the great disgust of the bystanders, and horror of the merchant. Then she demanded the reward from him and the merchant brought her home to give her the money. He was about to give her the large sum, when fortunately Hushiar also came up there, and seeing him deliver such a heavy purse to an abandoned woman, asked him what it was for. And when he knew the reason, he said :—"Stop, let us see whether it cannot be done more cheaply." Then going up to the square with the woman and his friend, he asked her to show the spot where she had performed her feat of brazen indelicacy. The spot was not very difficult to identify, and as there were still many spectators lingering there, they also corroborated her account and said :—"Hushiar, though we also strongly condemn the character of the woman, yet your friend must pay the wager, however dishonourable it may be for her to accept it. He had no business to accept the challenge." "Gentlemen," said Hushiar, "my friend is perfectly willing to pay the wager, but I have come to satisfy myself about the correctness of the account." Then taking a measure tape out of his pocket, Hushiar began to measure the sides of the square, and measuring also the spot where the feat was performed from the four sides, he found that it was not exactly the *middle* of the square, but somewhat nearer to one side than the other. Then turning to the people and the woman, he said "Woman, did you not promise to do this most shameful thing in the *middle* of the square ? And now, gentlemen, do you see that it is not the *middle*, but very far from it ? So has she not lost her wager ?" All were very much pleased at the ingenuity of Hushiar, and unanimously cried out :—"Yes, she has lost her wager." Then Hushiar addressing the woman, said :—"Thou vile creature, thou hast first done a very shameful deed, for which thou oughtst to be hanged, then thou falsely demandedst a heavy reward for thy misdemeanour, for which thou shouldst be heavily punished. Therefore give us ten thousand rupees or we drag thee before the king." The poor woman was obliged to pay the money to save her head, and was never again heard to say that she would cut capers in the middle of the public square. The friends shared the booty between themselves, and Hushiar again warned his comrade not to meddle with the muddle-headed citizens.

On the third day of his stay in the city of Janjal Nagari, Kam-Aql took a heavy oath not to go out, but to remain all day long in the house. So he did not stir a foot out of it. But finding that his beard had grown long, he sent for a barber to shave him; and when he arrived, asked him to do so, saying:—"Barber, trim me and I will pay you something for your trouble." The barber performed the office, and asked for the remuneration. The merchant then gave him two rupees, as his dues, and it was more than sufficient, but the barber did not accept it, saying:— "Sir, give me *something*, I want nothing but *something*." The merchant biting his lips, and cursing the thick-headedness of the barber, doubled the amount, but still the fellow would not touch the money, repeating; "I will accept nothing but *something*, give me the something which you promised." Poor Kam-Aql offered him by degrees so much as fifty rupees, but the man of the razor grew more and more obstinate and headstrong, and noisily cried out:—"Sir, I spit on your offer. Do you wish to tamper with my honesty? Do you think I will accept your bribe of fifty rupees, or for the matter of that fifty thousand rupees, and budge from my contract? Never, Sir, never, I will take nothing but *something*." The merchant was thinking what to do, when fortunately Hushiar came there and asked what was the dispute about. Kam-Aql told him the case, and then Hushiar turning to the barber, said:— "Friend, come early to-morrow morning and you will get your dues." The barber went away and Hushiar taking a cup of milk put a dead cricket in it, and kept it on a niche. When it was morning the barber returned to claim his fee, and Hushiar pointing to the cup, said, "Bring that cup of milk to me, I wish to drink it." The barber took down the

Plate VII.

" I have got *something*, I have got *something*."

vessel, and seeing the cricket floating in it, which, by the bye, had swollen by being soaked in the milk, involuntarily cried out: "Sir, do not drink it, there is *something* floating in it." "Ah, friend," said Hushiar, "that *something* is for you; give me the milk." The man taking the disgusting insect by the leg, went out very much pleased, showing it to all passers-by and crying out:—"I have got *something*, I have got *something*. I did not accept fifty rupees, but I have got at last my *something*." All who heard his story highly praised his prudence and veracity, and said that he was a true son of Janjal Nagari and had well maintained its credit.

The three days of stay of Kam-Aql had expired by this time, and Hushiar Khan told his guest:—"Friend, let us now go to your city. So you have realised the truth of the three sayings which I sold you some time ago. Now what do you fear from your friend?" The merchant replied:—"I am convinced that my cook has conspired with my friend Kam-Ikhlaq to rob me. I have promised to give my friend anything in my house on which he may first place his hand. What do you think that he will place his hand upon, but on my caskets of precious jewels? So I have come to implore you to save me from this calamity." Saying this the merchant wept bitterly in the anguish of his heart. Then Hushiar comforting him said:—"Let us start at once. Be not afraid; all will go well. As regards the three thousand rupees you gave me, I hope I have repaid more than enough during your three days' residence here. But to save my credit as a seller of maxims, riddles, proverbs, &c., I must help you out of this difficulty, of which I was the indirect and remote cause." The freinds then started on their journey, and reached the merchant's city.

When Hushiar came to the house of Kam-Aql, he told him to raise a spacious scaffold, fourteen feet high, in the middle of a *dalan* (square) and to arrange everything in his house on the structure. The merchant very soon had such a scaffold erected, and placed, in good order, everything which his house contained, on it. Then Hushiar told him to place his caskets on the top of all his other property. This was also done by the merchant. Then a wooden ladder just fourteen feet high, was placed perpendicularly on the ground touching the edge of the top of the scaffold, and all other means of ascending it were removed. Now the straight ladder was the only way of reaching the top and that also was almost impossible to scale. Then Kam-Aql sent for Kan-Ikhlaq, and when he arrived said :—"Behold on that platform displayed all the wealth of my house. Behold there boxes containing the richest diamonds, clothes and ornaments. There you might see also my cattle, horses and slaves. Go and select anything which you like. Kam-Ikhlaq looked on the ground and then on the scaffold and saw how high it was;—a slip from the ladder would instantly dash his brains out. Then also the ladder was so exactly perpendicular and placed on the edge without any support that the boldest hearts would have been daunted to try the ascent. But led away by obstinacy and blind through avarice, the faithless friend put one foot on the first step of the ladder, and catching hold of the next by his hands,

Plate VIII.

" You have got your wager,—won a ladder."

was going to ascend, when Hushiar caught him by the wrist and said :—"Desist, foolish and faithless friend. You have put your hand first on this ladder ; so take it away. You have got your wager,—won a ladder." The treacherous friend went away baffled and disappointed, carrying the ladder on his shoulders through the crowded town, and in the midst of the ridicule of all men.

THE STORY OF FOUR FRIENDS

Once upon a time there lived four friends. One was the son of a king, another of a goldsmith, the third of a pandit, and the fourth of a carpenter. The four friends used to wrestle together, and all were very brave and powerful. One day as they were wrestling, a giant came and made an enclosure of four walls around them, and challenged the four friends to try their strength on it by breaking it down. All tried in vain, but none succeeded, except the king's son, who broke the enclosure. On this the giant said: "You are the strongest of all, so go to Loha Garh or Iron Fort. There live a giant, and a beautiful princess worthy of you. Go there and kill the giant; so you will be known as the strongest man and get the most beautiful princess that ever breathed." The king's son was fired by the idea of getting her, and with the permission of his father at once started for the place. In the way he met his three friends, who accompanied him. They travelled on and on till they came to a lonely place where there was a well. Finding the place very pleasant and romantic they halted there. Three went out to hunt, and the fourth, the goldsmith's son, began to prepare food. As he was cooking, a giant came out of the well and said: "Give me something out of this food." The goldsmith's son replied, "I have not yet given to any *pir* or *faqir*, how can I give thee? Sit down; when my friends will come, thou shalt also get something." On this the giant caught him by the wrist and threw him aside and took away all the food. When the friends came they did not find any food ready. On learning the cause, another friend, the carpenter's son, volunteered to cook and fight the giant while the three went out to hunt. He met the same adventure. So did the third. At last the king's son volunteered to cook. The giant came out as usual and asked for food. The king's son said: "The bread has not been given as yet to *pir* or *faqir*, how dare you ask for it? Wait and you will get." On this the giant caught hold of the wrist of the king's son, and the latter caught hold of the other's hand, and there was a regular fight. At last, the king's son threw him down into the well and followed him into it and had a long fight there. When the giant, whose name was Tasma Shah, was perfectly subdued, he agreed to purchase peace by accompanying the prince in his journey and marrying his daughter to him. But the prince who was in search of the lady of Loha Garh, declined the latter offer, but negotiated the match for his friend, the goldsmith's son. So as soon as the marriage was solemnized, the three friends leaving the married couple behind started forward on their journey. Though they had lost one of their playmates, yet their number was not lessened, for the giant, Tasma Shah, true to his promise, accompanied them and proved of great service to them by his courage, devotion and fidelity to the prince. The three friends and the giant proceeded on their journey. They reached a city which was desolate, and where all the shops were closed. But in the midst of a large square there was only one living creature; she was a very beautiful girl with a basket full of flowers. On seeing them she began to weep and said: "Go away from this place. Do not stop here; for, this city is infested by a terrible giant who will soon come and devour you all." The giant Tasma Shah, who, by the bye, had assumed the shape of a man, for giants can put on any shape they like, said: "Never mind! we will stop here." Then they all stopped there for the night. The three friends being tired soon fell asleep, and Tasma Shah kept watch. As he was watching, he saw a very tall giant, whose head touched the sky, coming towards him; seeing him Tasma Shah rolled himself on the ground and resumed his orginal shape of a giant which was so long kept disguised under that of a man. He enlarged his height, and expanded his form to the utmost, but could not reach higher than the shoulders of the giant of the city. Both then began to fight, and there was a great fight between them, so that the walls of the city shook and trembled. At last Tasma Shah killed the other giant. By this time it was dawn. The carcase of the dead giant fell with a loud crash on the city and stretched for many a mile. When the king of the city learned the news of the giant's death from the women, he was very much astonished and pleased. For this giant was a very cruel one, and used to eat ten citizens every day, and had almost eaten away the whole city. The king searched out the four persons, and offered the hand of his daughter to Tasma Shah. But the latter generously recommended his friend, the pandit's son, instead.

So the second friend was married, and the two remaining friends and the giant, Tasma Shah, proceeded on their journey. They reached another city which was equally silent and desolate. They saw many pots full of milk and a very beautiful boy standing near them. On the friends

Plate IX.

" Both then began to fight."

enquiring why he was standing there alone, and why the shops were all closed, the boy said: "There comes a lion here, and he takes away daily a man and ten pots of milk." This day it is my lot to be devoured by the lion, and those pots, which you see, are for him. Do not stop here, but please go away." The three travellers gave hope to the boy, and promised to help him. So the king's son and the carpenter's son both slept, while Tasma Shah kept watch. At last, when it was midnight, the lion came with a loud roar. But as soon as Tasma Shah saw the lion, he ran towards him and killed him. When in the morning the vazir of the city passed on that side on his inspecting tour, he saw the dead lion and the four persons including the boy. The vazir asked them: "Who has killed the lion?" On learning the fact he took them before the Raja, who, in reward for this good service, gave in marriage his daughter to the carpenter's son. Then the king's son and the giant, Tasma Shah, proceeded on their journey towards Loha Garh, thus leaving one by one all their friends behind. At last they reached their destination. In that fort they saw a beautiful lady sitting on a tower. The giant took the prince on his back, and jumped into the fort and placed him before the beautiful lady. She strongly warned the prince to leave the fort, telling him that it was haunted by a giant. But the prince assured her that the horrible giant was already killed, and, so in fact it was, for in the meantime Tasma Shah had killed the giant of the fort. So the prince began to live with the lady. The prince lived in the tower, and Tasma Shah lived downstairs. The latter vowed never to go upstairs, which he held sacred, and received his food from the king's son who brought it down daily for him. The lady of the fort one day went out to bathe in an adjacent stream. She unfortunately lost her shoe in the stream. The shoe floating away touched the coast of a city where a Raja's son was bathing. The Raja's son took up the shoe, and finding it was a lady's shoe, preserved it carefully and fell in love with its unknown wearer. So he went home and sat in a corner moodily. When the king came and asked his son the reason, the prince said: "I will not live, if I do not get the person whose shoe this is, for my wife." The king hearing this, and finding that advice will be no remedy for the incurable malady of his son, promised to give him that lady in marriage. So the king called the witches of the place and asked them to bring the lady whose shoe it was. One of the witches who knew the spell to control streams, rivers and waters, undertook the task. So she chanted some charms, and dived into the stream and reached the fort of Loha Garh. She went near the tower and began to weep. The lady of the tower saw her, and calling her up hastily, was taken in by her specious tale of misery, and kept her as her servant. When the witch had remained there for some time, one day she advised her mistress to ask the prince the secret of his life and death. The lady of the fort, not fearing any mischief, asked the prince, and was told by him that his life lay in the brightness of his sword. As long as the sword remained bright and untarnished, he would be alive, but no sooner was it rusty than he would die. When

Plate X.

"The witch conveyed her to the Raja's son."

the foolish princess told this secret to the witch, the latter rejoiced very much in her heart. The evil woman was always on the look out for an opportunity to execute her wicked design. So one night when all had gone to sleep, the witch stole into the prince's room, took the charmed sword and put it into a burning furnace where it soon lost its brightness, and at that very moment the young prince lost his life. As soon as he was dead, the witch took up the sleeping princess and conveyed her under the stream to the Raja's son. The Raja and his son were very much pleased to get hold of the beautiful lady. But when the princess awoke, and found that she had been brought to this pass, she mustered all her courage, and her good sense soon devised a means of escape. She asked the Raja and his son to wait for a year, after which period she would marry the Raja's son. The Raja agreed to this, but kept the princess in close confinement in a strong fort.

Here Tasma Shah began to starve, for the prince being dead no one brought food for him. When he had passed a week without food he resolved to find out what was the matter. So once for all, breaking through his self-imposed vow, he went upstairs and with one glance took in the whole situation. He at once ran to the furnace, took out the sword and searched carefully whether any portion of it was bright or not. After a good search he found the tip of the sword still retaining its brightness, as it had been thrust into the earth and had not been burned. So Tasma Shah began to rub the sword, and after great efforts restored its brightness to the weapon and life to its prince. Then the two went out in search of the lost princess. They first got all the other friends together, *viz.*, the son of the pandit, &c. After great search the friends went to the city where the princess was kept a prisoner. They reached the city a few days before the expiry of the year of grace. Great preparations were being made for the coming marriage. They consulted together about the means of having a talk with the princess and giving news of their arrival. At last the pandit's son in the guise of an astrologer entered the fort, and under pretence of telling her fortune told the princess that the prince was in the city, and had devised some means for her release and told her what it was. A day before the marriage the princess said to the Raja that it was the custom of her family to float round the city in a golden ærial car with the bridegroom and the match-maker. The Raja, seeing that there could be no harm in indulging her in this whim, consented that she should have her wish, and sent his men to fetch such a car. In the meanwhile the giant, Tasma Shah, with the help of the goldsmith's son and the carpenter's son, had constructed such a car and brought it for sale to the Raja. The Raja bought the wonderful car and sat on it with the princess, his son, and the witch and began to move in the air round the city. When the princess told them to stop at a certain place and the car was stopped, the four friends, headed by Tasma Shah, jumped into the car and moving its hidden spring at once rose very high into the air. They then bound down the treacherous witch, the Raja and his son, and drowned them in the river for their wickedness and returned gloriously to their city.

THE STORY OF THE SEVEN PRINCES

In days gone by, long long ago, there was a king who had seven sons, all very brave, handsome and well-educated. They were all greatly loved by their father and were always treated with equal love. The old king, who was a wise man, never showed any undue preference for one to another, but distributed his love evenly amongst them all. They were dressed alike, equipped alike, and received the same allowances; and when they had grown up, separate places were assigned for their residence, which were built on one and the same plan and were all richly furnished. In fact if one saw one house it was as good as seeing the rest, so exact was the uniformity which prevailed in them all. Under such impartial and just treatment the princes lived very happily and loved one another dearly.

When they had reached marriageable age, the good king sent ambassadors all over the world to search for them seven brides, for equally distinguished beauty, talents and birth. The messengers of the king went all over the world, saw many princesses, but failed to find seven such brides. At last they all returned to the king and, prostrating themselves before His Majesty, said:—"Your most august Majesty, we have wandered over the *saptadvipa* (seven-islanded) world, crossed vast seas and high mountains, seen many kingdoms and empires, have been to courts as well as to cottages, but nowhere could we find seven brides of the same accomplishments, same qualifications, same temper and same beauty. In fact it is an impossibility to get brides for the princes worthy of them." When the king heard that the messengers had returned unsuccessful, he was greatly annoyed and perturbed. The grand vizier, who was a very sagacious statesman, finding that the king was becoming despondent and gloomy, cogitated in his mind to find some means to cure him of his melancholy, and hit upon the following plan to effect his purpose. He went up to the king and making a deep bow said with his palms joined:—"Your Majesty need not be so very anxious over the matter. Surely it is impossible to get seven such brides for the princes as Your Majesty would have, but when *tadbir* (human effort) fails wise men consign the matter to *taqdir* (destiny). Let your Majesty call the princes, and ask them whether they agree to select their partners by chance. If they do, then the matter can be very easily settled." The princes were at once sent for, and asked about it, and the princes, to the king's great surprise and relief, agreed. Whereupon they were conducted to the highest tower of the fort which overlooked the whole city and many a mile beyond. Then seven bows and seven arrows were placed before the princes and they were told to shoot in any direction they chose; each binding himself to marry a girl out of the house whereupon his arrow should fall, be she the daughter of a prince or peasant, noble or plebeian. Then the princes taking up the bows, shot arrows in various directions and all the arrows excepting that of the youngest prince fell on the houses of respectable and noble men. But the arrow shot by the youngest went out of the city and out of sight. Servants ran in all directions for the arrow and after much search found it sticking to the branch of a tree, on which was sitting a—she-monkey.

Great was the sorrow and regret of the king when he found that the youngest prince's arrow had made such an unfortunate descent. So he and the courtiers all advised the prince to try another chance, as a monkey cannot be an object of human conjugal affection. But the prince most respectfully said:—"Father, all the other princes, my brothers, have got good and handsome wives, for such was their destiny. I also took my chance and I have got what was destined for me. I do not complain; I am not envious. Do not advise me to break the solemn pledge which I took before I shot my arrow. Do not ask me to take another chance. Our lives are like grass, we come and go like shadows but the word is eternal and remains for ever. Let me not break my word. I know the monkey is no object of marriage, but know ye all that I shall never marry. I will go and fetch this monkey and bringing her home tend and foster her all my life." Having said so, he went out of the city and brought the monkey home.

All the six princes were married with great *eclat* and pomp. The city was all ablaze with lights, and fireworks, and sweet music discoursed in all the streets. The citizens decorated their houses with mango and plantain leaves, the merchants painted their shops anew; and exhibited their richest stores to the admiring gaze of the spectators who crowded the streets. There was merriment and rejoicing all over the city, and all were happy and cheerful. The youngest prince alone remained in his palace rather melancholy and sad. He had already placed a diamond collar round the neck of the monkey, and placing her on a chair covered with a rich velvet cushion addressed her thus:—"Poor monkey, thou art as uncared for as I am in this day of great rejoicing. But I shall make thy life happy, thy confinement a pleasant one. Do not pull so hard at the golden chain that binds thee, for this is thy only place of safety. Poor creature! art thou hungry?" Saying this he placed a golden dish full of most delicious fruits before her and bade her eat them. Thus was he wont to talk with her and pass his days neglected by all on account of his choice, which some called folly, others madness and others obstinacy.

The king daily took counsel with his viziers and nobles as to the means of curing the prince of his strange infatuation and bringing him to his senses, and inducing him to marry in some suitable family. But to all the advice of his father, brothers, councillors and friends the prince would invariably reply, "I have given my word; the word of a man is more durable than mountains, and dearer than wives and worlds." Thus months and months passed away, and there were no signs of the prince's changing his mind. On the contrary he appeared daily to become more and more fond of his monkey. The little creature also appeared as if she understood the prince, and showed her gratitude and love by every sign by which the lower animals can express their feelings.

At last the king one day called together all his seven sons and addressed them as follows:—"Dear children, I have seen you now all settled in your new abodes and living happily. Even you, my youngest, seem happy with your strange companion. You know, children, the happiness of a father consists in that of his sons and daughters, I wish to see my daughters-in-law and give them some presents." The eldest son coming forward said with great reverence :—"Your Majesty would confer the greatest happiness, if you condescended to dine with us to-morrow." The king gladly accepted the invitation. Great were the preparations that the eldest prince made for the royal reception and richly was the princess dressed, as much pains did the tire-women take to make her appear at her best. The king came at the proper hour to the palace of the prince, saw all the arrangements, and was greatly pleased with the entertainment provided for him by his son and his daughter-in-law. Then taking them both by the hands, he presented to the prince and princess precious and costly jewels, dresses and ornaments, and gave them, what was greater than all the wealth of the world, sound and wholesome advice as to how to live happily and long. When he had stayed there long enough, he returned to his palace.

The next day, he was invited by his second son to his palace, where also he was equally well regaled, if not better; and came out equally pleased. Thus did he visit one after another his six sons, and everywhere was he received with great respect, love and splendour by his sons and daughters-in-law. Now the turn came of the last son—the lord of the monkey—to invite his father. The poor prince was greatly troubled: for how could he invite his parent to a house whose mistress was a monkey, though that monkey was a more gentle, docile and affectionate creature than many a high-born lady ? So when he returned home, he went up to his pet and taking her up in his arms he addressed her saying :—

"Poor speechless partner of my sorrows and hopes, tell me what I shall do now! Oh how I wish that thou hadst a tongue to comfort me in this difficulty. All my brothers have shown their houses and their wives to father; what shall I show him when he comes here? I am even afraid of inviting him. How am I already ridiculed by all, and how much more ridicule will they heap upon me when I invite my father and present thee to him as my choice!" Thus did the prince go on for a long time talking with the monkey. He had unconsciously fallen into the habit of addressing her as if she were a rational creature. Nor could he have found a more patient and attentive listener than she, for she would sit with the gravest and most silent decorum all the while he poured forth his complaints, sighs and rhapsodies. Nor did he ever find her remiss in her diligence to please him, and he had often wondered at the extraordinary sagacity and instinct of the animal. But what was his astonishment when the monkey said :—"Do not grieve or be cast down. Go and invite your father as your brothers have done, but invite him with all his courtiers, army, and servants. Do as I entreat you." The Prince wondering and exclaiming "Lord, what mystery is this!" went out and invited the king, with his courtiers and army. The courtiers and the army were full of curiosity to know what the prince could mean by inviting them all; and much speculation was rife as to his motive, but all were unanimous in thinking that it was another example of his folly and that they would have another joke at his expense.

The Prince was sitting alone moody and thinking what

Plate XI.

The Shahjadi monkey.

to do next; when suddenly he heard a noise, and looking up saw that the monkey was calling him by her dumb gestures. The Prince sàid :—"Well my Shahzadi (for he used to call her jocularly by that name), you have brought me to a nice pass. I have invited the king and all at your bidding; and now where can I get men or money enough to give them a fitting welcome? Now tell me what I should do. Why don't you speak, have you lost your tongue?" But the monkey was as dumb as ever and the prince was almost persuaded to believe that he must have dreamt that the monkey had spoken. Then the prince again implored her to speak but without any effect, when he saw her holding a bit of broken pottery in her hands and earnestly making him signs to take it. The Prince coming up to her took the broken bit and saw to his greatest amazement the following words written in a most beautiful feminine hand on it :—"Do not fret at my silence. Go to the place whence you brought me, and throw this piece into the hollow trunk of the tree and wait for the reply."

The Prince hesitated for some moments as to whether he should comply with the written reply of the Shahzadi monkey, but at last made up his mind to do as requested and see what it would come to. He no longer doubted that there was some mystery behind it, and he hoped to solve it by following the direction of his pet. Though he more than once doubted whether his Shahzadi could be of any material help to him, he did not see any harm in going to the tree with the broken bit of pottery. So taking it up, he went out of the city, and after some search found out the tree. It was a remarkable tree—a large ancient Banyan many centuries old whose branches and pendent roots spread in a circle over half a mile in diameter and whose leaves and pillars formed many curious arbours and bowers. The trunk though hollow within was of the extraordinary thickness of a hundred yards in circumference. The prince going up to it, threw the bit into the hollow space and awaited the fruition of events. After some minutes a very beautiful lady of angelic form dressed in green came out of it, and asked the prince to follow her in, as the princess, the queen of the fairies, required his personal presence. The prince climbed up the tree, entered the hollow and after groping in the dark was soon ushered amidst a blaze of brilliant lights into a most picturesque and wonderful garden, at the end of which there was an imperial palace. The trees were all of living gold, and the leaves of sapphire and precious stones. They were all planted in rows and between them flowed streams of water of such a sweet scent that one might mistake it for *amrita* (nectar). It was so transparent and pure that even the rubies and diamonds in the bed of the stream and the wonderful fishes of silver moving therein were perfectly visible as if depicted in a mirror. *Bulbuls*, *koils*, nightingales and other singing birds kept up a perpetual music. A pleasing wind fraught with perfume blew through the alcoves and groves made by the trees. Even the light which illumined this underground world was of a strange and unique kind.

Every five minutes it changed from one hue to another and the prince at first thought that he was witnessing some wonderful display of fireworks. At the end of the garden there was a large tank whose waters were of golden hue and rose into the air in many a fountain and spout, and spread a pleasant coolness and fragrance all around. On the northern side of the fountain was a balcony of the whitest marble; it was a balcony having twelve doors called *Baradari*, to which the prince was conducted by a flight of stairs all of gold. Within the room the sight which met his wondering gaze filled him with inexpressible awe and astonishment. It was furnished with such taste and elegance as he had never before seen or imagined; but the greatest wonder of all which riveted his sight was a lady of incomparable and unapproachable beauty, sitting on a *masnad*. The prince remained long absorbed in admiration and contemplation of the beauty of this lady and did not dare announce his message. The lady beckoned him to take his seat and then in accents whose silver melody thrilled through his veins, said:—"Prince, I know your message; be not anxious. Go home and you will find everything ready by to-morrow morning to receive your royal father and company. I have ordered my servants to do everything." The Prince with a deep bow returned with greater amazement than before.

When he reached his palace, he gave an account of his subterranean journey to the Shahzadi. All the night he had no sleep, for he was thinking, over and over again, of the gorgeous scenes he had witnessed, and the beautiful lady whom he had seen. When it was morning he went out to see whether the Fairy had fulfilled her promise or not; but as he issued out of his palace a wondrous sight met his view. Where the night before there was nothing, now it teemed with life and bustle. There stood two long colonnades of trees stretching from his palace to the palace of the king. Rich and mellow fruits hung on the trees; and fresh streams of water flowed on both sides. A costly carpet of the most beautiful velvet embroidered with gold and silk was spread the whole length of the way from the palace of the prince to that of his father. At short intervals there rose triumphal arches, emblazoned with appropriate mottos and devices; while a row of various-coloured flags, banners, &c., fluttered and waved in the balmy air. Under the shades of the trees there were stalls and shops, where fruit, scents, sherbets, &c., were being sold; while on both sides were pitched tents and *kanats* within which went on diverse kinds of *tamashas* and amusements. Here and there might be seen groups of men, women, and children playing or listening to music and dancing. The farther the prince proceeded, the greater and more pleasing were the surprises that burst on his view, so much so that he was well-nigh bewildered at what he saw and heard.

Then he returned and entered his palace where fresh wonders called forth his admiration. The house which an hour before he had left almost silent was now all activity and noise. Servants and lackeys in rich dresses, passed and repassed the halls, corridors and rooms. Large preparations were being made for receiving a company of ten thousand persons or so. Golden dishes and plates groaning under the weight of the nicest foods exhaled sweet odour all through the house. The preparations were all on a scale befitting gods and *peris*. Grand chandeliers of the purest quartz and precious stones hung from the roofs, and bands of musicians played delightful airs on various instruments, stringed and vocal. Here and there hung rich festoons of flowers, and filled the whole palace with a delightful perfume.

In the meantime, as the Prince was observing all these busy and wonderful preparations, a servant in gorgeous livery came running in and announced that the king with his courtiers, &c., was coming. The prince at once hastened out and conducted his father and other guests to the Diamond Hall, which was the most wonderfully decorated of all. There a sumptuous repast was served to them ; and when the feast was over, the prince told the guests to take away with them all the golden dishes and the diamond-cups in which they had taken their food. Their admiration grew great at the unparalleled liberality of the prince.

Then the king addressing his son said:—"Dear Prince, I do not wish to know whence you got all these riches which far surpasses all that I possess ; nor am I anxious to know who prepared these delicious dishes the equal of which I had never tasted before in my memory, but I am desirous of seeing the partner you have chosen for your life, so that I may bless her." The prince, bowing low and saying "your commands shall be obeyed," went into the inner apartments in search of the monkey. He had feared this crowning ridicule all the while, but what could he do? He must show his monkey to them all. In fact the king had hit upon the stratagem of visiting his sons, as a means of curing the youngest one of his obstinacy and opening his eyes to the folly which he was committing in sticking to the monkey.

The prince went slowly towards the room where the Shahzadi was kept; and coming to it, opened the doors: when a dazzling lustre almost struck him blind, and the whole apartment was a blaze of light. In the midst of this luminous flood, and on a gorgeous throne sat the Peri whom the prince had seen in his visit to the tree. The Prince looked on every side for his monkey but it was nowhere. The Peri seeing the bewilderment of the prince said:—"Prince, since I saw you last in the cave, I have thought of nothing else but you. I have sent away the Shahzadi monkey and come to offer my hand to you. Do you accept me?" The Prince hearing the fate of his pet, shed bitter tears and said most angrily, his voice choked with sobs:—"Cruel lady, what have you done? I have plighted my faith to my monkey and do you ask me to forsake her and break my solemn pledge for a pretty face like yours? I had a better idea of you, when I first saw you, but I now find I was mistaken; Ah me!" Then the Peri with a smile, which the prince could not understand, said:—"Prince, if my beauty does not move you, let at least considerations of gratitude have some influence with you. See what pains I have taken to prepare this feast for your father and guests, a feast which no human being has ever enjoyed before and which is peculiar to our race of beings. Prince, be mine, and you shall have all the riches and the pleasures of the world at your command." The prince indignantly replied:—"Lady, I never asked these things of you, nor do I know what infernal plot is this to deprive me of my monkey. Restore me my Shahzadi, and I will serve you my whole life as your slave to pay off this heavy debt." Having said this the prince knelt down before the Peri. Then the Peri coming down from her throne and with a smile of ineffable sweetness, respect and love, said :—"Prince, behold in me your Shahzadi. I had taken the form of the monkey to test your faith and sincerity. My monkey's skin lies in that corner." And the prince looked in the direction pointed out, and saw in fact the skin of the Shahzadi monkey. O, who can now describe the happiness of the prince?

Then the Peri, taking hold of the prince's hand, raised him to the throne and both seated themselves on it. The Peri then thrice repeated "arise, arise, arise," and the throne rose into the air and floated to the Diamond Hall where the guests were assembled. The Prince then presented the Shahzadi to his father. The astonishment of the king and the guests might well be imagined. Those who had come to see a monkey and to laugh at the prince, now stood dumb and confounded. The king gave more than usual presents to his new daughter-in-law, and the whole country was soon ringing with praises of the truthfulness of the prince and the beauty of the Peri.

The other princes on seeing the good fortune of their youngest brother became envious, and conspired how to encompass his ruin. So one day they said to the prince :—"Brother, your wife is a Peri belonging to a race of beings proverbial for their fickleness and want of purpose. We have heard that you have got the skin which the Peri had assumed before. Why do you keep it with you? God knows when the Peri may change her mind and again become a monkey. Better destroy it." The Prince thought over this for some time, and falling into the snare, took out the skin, and going to a blazing furnace threw it in.

At once there arose loud screams of "I burn, I burn, I am roasted, I am roasted," and the Peri came out in the midst of a column of fire and rushed out of sight crying as before. The Prince was struck with horror and alarm and ran home to see what was the matter. The sight which met him confirmed his saddest misgivings, and he found that the whole palace, the Bazar, and everything which the Peri had brought with her, had vanished with her disappearance.

Then the prince began to bemoan his folly and misfortune. The king and the ministers consoled him, saying: —"What love can there exist between the son of a man and the daughter of the air? You must not grieve for her, she was no human being; she was of the air, aerial, and has vanished into it. Leave off weeping for her." But the prince was disconsolate and would not listen to any advice. The king fearing that the prince in his excess of sorrow might lay violent hands upon himself or run away, stationed a strong guard to watch over his proceedings and movemets. Thus the prince became a prisoner in his own house, and chafed at the captivity which prevented him from searching out the Peri.

One day, however, he gave the slip to his guards and went out of the city. He repaired straight to the old banian tree hoping to find some trace of his Peri there; but when he reached the spot there was no tree standing, but instead a large heap of ashes. So he went away from that place weeping and striking his forehead. For days and

Plate XII.

" I burn, I burn, I am roasted, I am roasted."

days he went on, eating the fruit of the trees, drinking water from the pools and sleeping under the canopy of heaven and crying, Shahzadi, Shahzadi. He crossed large forests, and travelled farther and farther and was very sore of feet and weary of spirit. At last one day he came upon a man who was standing on one leg and was crying :— "Once have I seen thee, appear once more." The Prince saw that the man was in equally bad plight with him; his body was emaciated, his eyes had sunken into their orbits, his limbs had become wiry, his unkempt hair and unshaven beard hung in bushy growth above and around: in fact he was a living skeleton. Struck with his appearance, as well as the words he uttered, the prince asked him to tell him his story. The man replied :—"Know, O kind-hearted traveller, that I am the son of a king. I had come out to hunt, and had straggled away from my retinue, when I saw a very beautiful and handsome lady passing this way. She was all a blaze of fire, and was crying :— 'I burn, I burn; I am roasted, I am roasted.' Since then have I been standing here in this sad state." Saying this the man heaved a deep sigh and cried out :—"Once have I seen thee, once more appear." Then the Prince said :—"Ah me, I am the unfortunate wretch who has burned that lady, I am the unlucky husband of that person. What way did she take?" The man pointed him out the direction. The Prince was about to go away, when he said :— "Traveller, I shall always pray that you may succeed in your search. But when you recover her, kindly show her once more to me. And that you may better remember me, take this iron rod as a token. It has this peculiar virtue that it obeys the commands of its possessor. Tell it to beat any person, and it will at once go wherever that person may be, and pound him to a jelly. It might be of great help to you in times of danger." The Prince took the rod, and, thanking the man for his kindness, went his way.

For months and months again he travelled through dreary and dangerous deserts raising echoes through the air of "Shahzadi, Shahzadi." He crossed vast tracts of burning sand and the soles of his feet were all a heap of blisters and sores. After suffering incalculable hardships and troubles, he saw a grove of trees—an oasis in the midst of that burning marl. He entered it, parched with thirst, and refreshed himself at a cool and murmuring stream. He sat down there for a while, when most delightful music fell on his ears as if some one was playing on a guitar. He went in search of the musician, and found him in the middle of the grove. He was a good looking youth of thirty or so and was absorbed in playing on the guitar. So sweet was the music, that birds and beasts had thronged round him in a circle and stood transfixed as if they were pictures on canvas, without motion, without even so much as breathing. All were in a trance. When the young man finished his music he heaved a deep sigh and groaned out loudly :—"Once have I seen thee, once more appear." The prince was struck with this exclamation and asked him who he was. The musician said :—"I am the son of a merchant. As I was passing by this way, I saw a most beautiful lady rushing by, who was all ablaze and crying :—'I burn, I burn, I am roasted,

Plate XIII.

"When the young man finished his music he heaved a deep sigh."

I am roasted.' Since then I am here. It is about six months ago." Then the prince discovered himself to the merchant's son and told him the object of his travels, telling him that he was the husband of that lady. Then the musician gave him the guitar which had the wonderful property of charming every living thing that heard it. The prince thanking him, and promising him to show him his Peri if he succeeded in his enterprise, took his leave and went forward.

Many insurmountable obstacles had the courageous prince to encounter and many difficulties to cope with but still his resolution never wavered, nor did his brave heart ever falter for a moment. He pushed on through dangers which would have daunted the most valiant, and hardships before which heroes themselves would have quailed with fear. After many months he came to a mountain whose tall peaks kissed the sky. His path lay over the mountain, whose precipitous sides and deep chasms sent a thrill of terror through the hearts of the beholders. Perpetual snow covered its top with a mantle of white. The prince began to ascend the mountain, whose slippery surface gave but little foothold to him. But still he went on till he reached a very high peak where he heard some one crying in a plaintive voice, "once have I seen thee, once more appear." The prince looked all round to find the person who was making this sad moan in such a place. But he could not see any one, though he found the spot whence the sound was proceeding. Then, raising his voice he said aloud :— "Whoever makest this sad lament in this solitary place, show thyself to a brother in affliction." No sooner had he made this exclamation, than he saw before him a youth, pale and haggard, and uttering the dolorous lament. On being asked, who he was, he said :—"About a year ago, I saw a very beautiful lady, all in a flame, pass by this way. She was crying 'I burn, I burn, I am roasted, I am roasted.' Since then have I been here crying and waiting for her." The prince said :—"I am that unfortunate wretch who has burned and roasted her. I am now going to find her and cure her if she be alive." The man of the mountain presenting a cap to the prince said :—"Prince, take this cap; it has the wonderful property of making one invisible when put on, as you saw me just now. If might be of some sevice to you in your travels." The prince accepted the gift, and thanking him for the favor went forward.

Higher and higher did he ascend the mountain and more and more difficult became the passage. The cold began to pierce him through and through, he shivered all over, his blood was freezing and his breathing becoming short and difficult. Enduring all these sufferings with patience, he rose up and up till he came to a temple. It was a building of snow, the pillars of snow, the shafts, the roofs, all were of snow, solid and compact. He entered it and the inside was warm and pleasant. Within the room was a Yogi immersed in trance, and seated on the air many feet above the ground, without any support. A halo of light surrounded his head and his whole body was resplendent. The prince stood with joined palms, with awe and reverence, in deep adoration of the holy saint. After some hours the Yogi opened his eyes and looking straight on the prince said, "Young man, I know thy history. The object of thy search is the daughter of the king of the Peris, whose mansion is on the top of Koh-kaf (Mount Caucasus). She is still alive but very ill. Take this pot of balsam; it has the virtue of healing the most dangerous burns. Take also this pair of wooden slippers, which will transport thee wherever thou likest." The prince took the pot of balsam and the wooden slippers with many thanks and then wearing the latter desired to reach the land of the king of the Peris, when, behold! he at once rose high in the air, and was carried with incalculable speed through the atmosphere to the region of the Peris. The prince then alighted outside the city, in a lonely and out of the way place.

Then putting on his cap he entered the city; and began to see the wonders of fairyland. Such were the virtues of the cap that no one saw him, but he saw all. The city was grand and glorious, laid out in a regular plan. The people were a strange and queer sort of individuals, who, though having the outlines of men, were not exactly human. They were all very fair and good-looking. The prince went on observing all, and came to the palace. As he was invisible, he entered boldly by the main gate, and went straight to the inner apartments where the Peri, his wife, was. He found her stretched on a bed, feeble and ill.

The prince then came out of the city and dressing himself in the garb of a holy saint took off his cap, and began to play on the guitar. The music rolled on and on over the waves of the air, and sent a thrill of delight throughout the whole city. The fairy people all rushed out to hear this enchanting harmony. The news of the wonderful performance on the guitar by a yogi soon reached the Peri-king. The king came to the spot to verify the report and was charmed with the music. Then falling on his knees before the prince the king of the Peris said:—"Holy Saint, vouchsafe to hear the prayers of thy humble servant. My daughter is lying on a sick-bed, burned by some accursed son of man. Cure her, O mighty Saint, for she is the light of my eyes, and the hope of my old age. Cure her, and I promise to grant whatever boon your holiness may ask." The supposed yogi replied:—"King, we are servants of God and do not enter the threshold of any creature. Bring thy daughter here, so that I may pray for her and cure her." The king of the Peris said again most humbly: —"Most holy Sir, my daughter is too ill to move. It would be her death to bring her here. So condescend to accompany me to my humble dwelling and bless it with the dust of thy sacred feet." When the prince was sufficiently entreated to keep up appearances of his being a very pious and holy saint, he at last agreed to accompany the king, and was carried with great honor, in a golden chair borne by the Peris, to the palace of the king. He was carried to the female apartments and was conducted to the room where his wife was. She was sleeping, when the prince arrived; so he took out that balsam and told the waiting women to apply it on the burns. No sooner was it applied than she sat up on her bed, perfectly cured. At once the cry went forth through the city that the great yogi had performed a miracle.

As the Peri saw the prince she at once recognised him, and was going to call him by his name, when he signed to her not to reveal their relationship lest it might bring on trouble. When the king heard that his daughter was cured, great was his delight and gratitude, and he said :—"Holy Sir, ask any boon." The prince, who had waited for this moment, said :—"Most mighty king, grant me thy daughter in marriage. This is my prayer." The king was enraged at the audacity of the holy mendicant, and called out most furiously to his attendants :—"Seize that presumptuous wretch and throw him into prison. His insolence has cancelled all the gratitude which I owed him." As soon as the officers came to arrest him the prince put on his cap and became invisible. In the meantime he ordered his rod to give a sound thrashing to the false king and his courtiers. At once up flew the obedient rod, and began to fall in heavy blows on the backs of all. Great was the consternation of the fairies on thus being thrashed by a rod moved by no visible hands; and the king at last supplicated for mercy, saying :—"Great saint, have mercy on us; we have erred through ignorance. Show thyself to us and I solemnly promise that thou shalt get whatever thou desirest." Then the prince made himself visible and said :—"I regret that I had to use this iron argument to convince thee of my power and strength. Now give me thy daughter with three of the most beautiful damsels of thy realm to attend her and the costliest diamonds and jewels from thy treasury as a penalty for thy breach of promise. Give me also a flying car which Peris only know how to make, and let it transport us to my father's kingdom." Then the king of the Peris at once brought his daugther attended by the three fairies and seated on a gorgeous throne. Then the prince also sat on the throne and they flew back through the air to their country. He stopped on his way to meet the Yogi and other friends who had helped him with the cap, the guitar and the rod. They were all very much pleased at seeing the prince return with his Peri. At the request of the prince, all of them except the Yogi, accompanied him to his kingdom, where they were married with great pomp to the three Peris who attended the princess ; and they all lived happily.

What became of the envious brothers ? When the king, their father, came to know of it, he was very much enraged and disinherited them all, and would have thrown them into dungeons ; but the youngest prince interceded for them and procured their pardon, and at his request suitable pensions were settled on them.

Plate XIV.

" They flew back through the air to their country."

THE STORY OF PRINCE SHAMSHER JANG

There was a king who had no son. He called all the holy men of his realm, and asked them to pray for him for a male child. The prayers of the holy men found acceptance, and a very beautiful boy was born to the king. Great was the joy of the king on seeing the dearest hope of his life realised, and large gifts were made to sacred shrines and temples, and there was great rejoicing throughout the kingdom. Then the king called the astrologers, and requested them to cast the nativity of the child. They all predicted many auspicious things of the infant prince,—that he would be the strongest among men, and very fortunate in all his adventures; that a happy conjunction of the stars shed its genial influence on his birth, and that everything augured long life and happiness. But the king, the holy men added, should take one precaution, which was that the prince should never be permitted to see the face of the sun before he had completed his fourteenth year, and that he should, therefore, be brought up in a strong fort whose walls should be of massive iron, seven feet thick. The king did as the astrologers and the wise men of the realm told him to do. When the fourteen years had expired, the prince, who, by the bye, was named Shamsher Jang, one day struck the wall with his fist, and so severe was the blow that the seven feet thick iron wall broke into two, as if blown up by a mighty cannon, and fell in pieces on the ground. The young prince issued out of his prison-house, and went forth towards the east.

In the way he saw a man digging the hot parched earth with a spade. Shamsher Jang asked him, "What are you doing, my good friend ? You must be very strong indeed to be able to dig with your spade such a burning and rocky soil as this." The labourer replied :—"Young man, I am no doubt known as the strongest among my class, but we have a prince called Shamsher Jang who has broken a seven feet thick iron wall with his fist. He is stronger than I." Then the prince made himself known to the labourer, saying :—"I am the prince of whom you speak." On this the earthdigger knelt down, and kissing the ground said :— "Henceforth, I acknowledge myself as your inferior; I offer myself as your disciple and slave, and will accompany you whithersoever you may travel." The prince accepted the labourer, whose name was "Weakbody," and proceeded on his journey. When they had travelled some distance they found themselves about noon one day in a spacious maidan, in the midst of which was standing a man with a bow who was crying out :—"Take care, take care, move aside, move aside, or you will be pierced through by yonder arrow." The prince asked him what he meant by this nonsense. The man replied :—"Sir, my name is Weak-sight, and I shot an arrow fourteen years ago at yon star in the zenith, and it is just returning, so I warned you lest it might injure you in its fall." The prince and Weakbody strained their eyes to see the arrow and the star, but could see neither. They waited there expecting to see the fall of the wonderful arrow which had been shot fourteen years ago and after an hour they saw a burning meteor fall on the ground with tremendous velocity and pierce the earth

Plate XV.

Weak-sight awaiting the fall of his arrow.

many a yard deep. It was the arrow which Weak-sight had shot fourteen years ago, and which he had described falling from the height of a thousand miles.

On seeing this the prince said :—"Friend, you must be the strongest man to shoot an arrow so far, and the farthest-sighted to see it from such a distance." Weak-sight replied :—"Sir, up to a short time ago, I deemed myself the strongest of men. But we have got a prince called Shamsher Jang, who has broken down with his fist a seven feet thick iron wall. He is my superior in strength." Hearing this the prince answered :—"I am Shamsher Jang, of whom you speak." On this Weak-sight also became the disciple of the prince and accompanied him on his journey.

The prince and his two companions went onward, meeting with no adventure till they reached a very delightful garden full of many a tree laden with fruits. In the middle of the garden on a raised dais was sitting a man, strong and glowing with health and vigour. He appeared to be absorbed in the contemplation of the fruits, and, as soon as he perceived the prince and his followers approaching, cried out :—"Away, you people, away. Have you come to beg these fruits of me ? Have you come to starve me ? I won't give you a single fruit, or even a single branch, root or leaf, however hard you may beg." Struck with this address, the prince replied :—"Sir, you need not be afraid of our begging of you any fruit. We are not hungry. But explain to us, good Sir, what you will do with these countless fruits. There is no city near where you can sell them, and we see no one to share these with you in this lonely place." The man of the garden replied :—"Sir, you appear to be a gentleman from your speech and conduct, as you have not come to beg for fruits; but if you knew me, you would not think me churlish, as my speech might have led you to imagine. Know, Sir, my name is Weak-appetite. I planted these trees exactly fourteen years ago; and have been tending them so long fasting all these fourteen years. Now they have brought forth fruit as you see,—mangoes, apples, annanas, pears, berries, &c., and I am awaiting the hour of my long deferred repast; and in fact the hour is not far distant, when I will eat up not only the fruits, but also the trees themselves, branches and all. Wait and you will see whether I lie, or speak the truth." The prince sat down with his friends on the dais and just as it struck the hour of noon the gardener fell on the trees like a hungry giant and soon left not a shrub standing. The prince, seeing this wonderful feat, accosted the gardener, saying:—"You are the strongest of all men." The gardener said:—"No, Sir, our prince, Shamsher Jang, is the stronger of us two. He has broken a seven feet thick iron wall with his fist." The prince said:—"I am he of whom you speak." Weak-appetite fell on the ground, acknowledged the prince as his master and accompanied him in his travels. They went on and on till they came to a large tank, on the banks of which was seated a man looking anxiously at the water. The prince and his three companions approached him and asked, "Why are you sitting here?" The man replied:—"I dug this tank exactly fourteen years ago, and have been ever since sitting here and awaiting its filling up by the rains. It has just filled up to the brim and I am going to drink it all off. My name is Weak-thirst." The prince observed:—"You must be the strongest of men to drink off such a large tank." Weak-thirst replied :—"No, Sir, our prince, Shamsher Jang, is the stronger. He has broken down an iron wall seven feet thick with one blow of his fist." The prince then made himself known to Weak-thirst and the latter thereupon became his follower and accompanied him. The prince tarried there for a while and then proceeded on his wanderings with his friends. They came to a large city where there were many shops and large buildings and palaces. The shops were full of every kind of merchandise and contained all that comfort or luxury could demand. They were all open, and the varieties of sweet delicacies exhibited on the stalls for sale whetted the appetite of the travellers, although it needed no whetting, hungry as they were after their long journey. But, strange to say, none of the shops had any keeper, there were none to sell, nor any to buy—the whole city was desolate and lifeless. The prince and his companions searched one shop after another, but found no human being. So they helped themselves freely to everything that pleased their fancy and ate and drank to their heart's content. They remained there for the whole day and when it was night they entered one of the most spacious and well furnished of the untenanted palaces and laid themselves down to rest. When it was about midnight, a monster, fourteen inches high, carrying in his hand an iron rod fourteen yards long, entered the desolate city, shaking the houses with his heavy tread, and roaring out: "I have eaten all the men of this city, but now again I smell human flesh. Come out, ye rogues, that I may eat you." Shamsher Jang hearing this menace came out with his drawn sword and facing the dwarf coolly said:—"What dost thou brag of, fellow? Know I am Shamsher Jang, who has broken an iron wall, seven feet thick, with one blow of his fist. Come, fight with me." Hearing this the dwarf, whose name was Gootia Deo, or little gaint, at once fell on the ground and kissing the dust of the prince's feet, replied with great humility, "I acknowledge myself your servant and slave. Be you my master, for you are my superior in strength. I also will accompany you in your travels. Deign to accept my services." The prince was, of course, glad to receive such a desirable enforcement to his company and accepted Gootia Deo as his follower and fellow-traveller. Then the six friends leaving behind that city without citizens proceeded forward.

They travelled for months till they came to another large and well-peopled city. They took up their lodgings in an inn outside the city walls. Their landlord was a kind and cheerful host and welcomed them most heartily. The travellers had reached the inn in a very happy moment, for it was the day on which the eldest and only son of the host was going to be married to a beautiful and rich heiress. The six travellers also joined merrily in the festivities of the day. When the marriage ceremony was over and a priest had tied the indissoluble knot between the bride and the bridegroom and when felicitations were pouring in upon the happy couple from all sides, a king's officer in red entered the inn and calling aside the host whispered something in his ears. The man gave a loud scream and fell in a deadly swoon on the ground and wailings and lamentations rose on all sides. The prince and his companions wondered at this sudden change and asked a marriage guest to explain to them what the king's officer could have whispered which caused such wailing and lamentation in the house where a moment before all were so happy and gay. The marriage guest replied with a deep sigh :—"Know, Sirs, that about fourteen years ago a very horrible calamity befell our city. A terrible giant came here and began to spread havoc wherever he went. He began to swallow and devour whatever he could catch hold of. The citizens began to abandon the city and at last the king was forced to make peace with the cruel monster. It was agreed that the king should supply the giant daily with forty tons of bread, ten tons of ghee and one human being. So one of us is daily devoured by the giant and to-day the lot has fallen on the bridegroom just married, and the king's officer came to inform the host of this. When Shamsher Jang learned the cause of the grief of his landlord he at once resolved what to do. So going up to the company, he said :—"Gentlemen, you need not be saddened, but go on with your festivities. I will willingly go to this giant in place of the bridegroom, and help to rid your fair city for ever of this plague." Thus raising with his promise the damped spirits of the company, the prince went up with his companions to the place where the giant used to come for his food. He found there already four carts loaded with sweetmeats, cakes, and bread and one cart full of ghee. So the prince with his five friends began to keep watch, and when it was about midnight, a loud roar like that of thunder was heard, and a giant, whose head touched the sky, made his appearance. The five friends who had promised to back up the prince, ran into the carts and hid themselves under the loads of bread and butter as soon as they saw the hideous and frightful monster. But Shamsher Jang undaunted, though alone, awaited with perfect composure and with drawn sword the approach of the giant. As soon as the giant had drawn near, the prince suddenly attacked him and separated his head in a moment from the trunk. Then cutting off the nose and the ears of the giant and putting them into his pocket, he returned to his friends and called them to come out of their recesses, as the gaint was no more. As soon as they heard that the giant was killed they all jumped out and every one began to brag of his great courage. Weak-thirst said addressing the prince, "Master, master, shall I drink off the whole blood of this rogue of a gaint ?" Weak-sight not to be left behind his friend came forward and said :—"Master, shall I blow off the carcass with one arrow to a distance of a thousand miles ?" Weak-appetite also came forward and said :—"Order me prince, that I may devour this carcass whole and intact." So everyone began now, when the danger was over, to vaunt of his might and strength. But the prince calmly said :— "Friends, there is no necessity now of your valour and courage this night, so let us go back and have some sleep before it is day." So the prince and his friends returned to the inn and slept soundly.

Here, when it was day, the news rerched the king that the gaint was no more. His Majesty hearing this happy news issued a proclamation ordering the gaint-killer to come forth and receive the reward of his valour, *viz.*, the hand of the king's daughter and sovereignty over half the

Plate XVI.

Shamsher Jang attacks the giant.

kingdom. The greed of this rich reward raised a host of claimants, each of whom swore that he had killed the giant. So the good monarch found himself in a dilemma, but the vizier soon helped him out of the difficult, saying :—"Your Majesty, when walking round the city this morning I happened to see the dead body of the giant. Observing the carcass with attention I found that the ears and the nose were missing. So if any of these claimants be the real giant-killer, he will be able to produce the missing nose and ears and that will solve the difficulty."

So when the king called upon them to produce the missing nose and ears, all failed except the prince, Shamsher Jang. So the king dismissed the others with a sharp reprimand: and offered his daughter and half his kingdom to the prince. But Shamsher Jang declined the offer with thanks and asked the king to confer the great favor of his daughter's hand on Weak-body, and to divide the offered half of his kingdom among his five companions. The king granted the request of the prince, and the latter saw his friend Weak-body married to the Princess and his other friends enthroned as kings of five several kingdoms.

Then the prince took leave of the king and his friends, and went forward on his journey accompanied only by the faithful Gootia Deo. After months of travel and great hardships, the two friends reached a large and beautiful city. They entered the town and walked through it doing justice to all its sights, seeing its splendour and riches displayed in its well-stocked shops, and well-furnished houses. At last they came to a palatial building which outshone all others in its magnificence and grandeur, and stood surrounded by houses like a king among his courtiers. The walls of the house were of pure gold, set in with diamonds and other precious stones. Never had the travellers seen such a glorious and imposing sight. They entered the portico, and were struck with wonder and dismay on seeing a human skeleton in military accoutrements standing on either side of the entrance and a drum in the middle. On enquiring of the people what it meant, they learned that the house belonged to an heiress, the daughter of a rich merchant. She had taken a vow not to marry any person who could not fulfil four conditions; these skeletons being the bleaching remains of the unsuccessful lovers. Hearing this the prince gave a loud succession of blows on the drum, and made the palace ring with the noise, thus announcing the arrival of another candidate for the heiress' hand to the inmates of the house. Hearing the loud drumming, the merchant's daughter sent her maid-servant to enquire who might be the daring person who had beaten the drum so loud. The servant soon returned conducting in the prince, Shamsher jang. When the merchant's daughter saw the prince and found him good-looking, brave and well-spoken, she inwardly prayed that he might come out successful from the trial. The prince was no less charmed with the beauty, grace and intelligence of the merchant's daughter, and asked her the four conditions which must be fulfilled. She replied:— "Prince, the conditions are these: first, I have been preparing food for the last fourteen years and it is stored up in yonder house. It must all be eaten up at once by a single person. Secondly, that tank which you see in the middle of the palace has been filled by the rains of fourteen summers. It must be drunk off by a single person. Thirdly, on your left you see another tank; it is of hot water, which has been boiling by a perpetual fire underneath these fourteen years; some one must bathe in it for an hour. Fourthly, I have a cousin living five thousand miles from here. She must be brought here in a single day. These are the four conditions; now, can you fulfil them?" The Prince replied that he would try; but asked fifteen days' leave for the purpose. Taking the lady's leave, he came out of the house, and going up to Gootia Deo, who was waiting outside, sent him to fetch all his friends whom they had left behind. The dwarf at once started on his errand and gave the message of the prince to his late travelling companions and followers.

No sooner had they received the prince's message than they started on their journey, and before the fortnight had expired, they presented themselves before their master. Prostrating themselves before the prince, they said:— "Master, we can never forget the kindness which you have shown us, and can never repay the deep debt of gratitude under which we lie. Tell us how we can be of any service to you." The prince told them that their respective powers would soon be put to the test, and that they could be of the greatest service to him in his present emergency. He then related to them his encounter with the merchant's daughter and the four conditions, which he must fulfil or lose his life. The friends reiterated the proffer of their services, and when the appointed fifteen days were over they all accompanied the prince to the house of the merchant's daughter. When the prince and his friends were ushered into the presence of the lady, she asked :—"Are you ready to perform your promise?" The prince replying in the affirmative, the lady pointed to the house full of the fourteen years' acumulation of food and said, "Eat that up". The prince addressing Weak-appetite said:—"Now is the time to show the capacity of your stomach; fall upon the mountain of food." Weak-appetite replied :—"Master, shall I make a *sip* or a *sup?*" The prince who did not understand what his friend meant by the two words, asked him to explain himself. The other replied:—"Dear Master, by *sip* I mean the eating away of the food alone stored here; by *sup* is meant the eating up of the food together with the baskests, dishes, cups, tables, glasses, and the room containing it." The prince said :—"Friend, let it be *sup* then."

By this time the news had spread that wonderful feats of eating and drinking, bathing and walking were to be witnessed at the house of the rich lady, and thousands thronged the courtyard to see the performances. Great and deafening were the shouts of "Wah!" "Wah!" which the citizens raised when they saw Weak-appetite take hold of large sacks full of food, put them into his mouth and thrust them down his throat by an iron rod. Soon he emptied the house of its food, and began swallowing the dishes, cups, &c. But the lady fearing lest all her precious furniture should find room in Weak-appetite's stomach, stopped the havoc, declaring that she was satisfied. Then the prince turning to Weak-thirst said:—"Friend, dry up yonder tank." The friend replied:—"Dear Master, shall I make

Plate XVII.

Weak-appetite shows his feats of eating.

a *nip* or a *nup?* "What do you mean by these words, my friend?" asked the prince. Weak-thirst replied:—"Master, *nip* is the simple drinking off of the water, and *nup* the drinking off of the water together with four yards deep of the mud and earth underneath and surrounding it." The prince replied: "Let it be *nup*." Then Weak-thirst fell upon the tank and drank off the whole water together with the mud, fountains, marble, ghats, banks, &c. The shouts and cheers of the spectators echoed back from the sky. Then the prince addressing Weak body said:—"Friend, enter yon tank of hot water." Weak-body replied: "Shall I bathe in the fashion of a *lip* or a *lup?*" On being asked by the prince to explain himself, he said:—"Dear Master, *lip* is the method of simple bathing in this hot water for an hour or so. *Lup* is the process of bathing in this hot water as well as in the fire that heats it." The prince said:—"Let it be *lup* then." Then Weak-body plunged into the burning waters and swam and dived and played a hundred tricks therein for a full hour, and then bursting open with his foot the floor of the tank entered the furnace beneath and remaining in it for an hour came out amidst the applause of the bystanders.

Then the prince said to Weak-sight:—"Friend, look to the four quarters and see where is the cousin of this lady at this moment." Weak-sight did as he was asked to do, and after surveying the four-quarters of the globe carefully, replied:—"She is at this moment exactly five thousand miles due north from this place sitting in a delightful garden." The prince then asked the dwarf Gootia Deo to fly and fetch her. The Deo went there with the speed of lightning and entering the garden presented himself before the lady and gave her the message that she was required at her cousin's, the merchant's daughter. The lady asked the dwarf to sit down and take some refreshments ; he agreed to the proposal most gladly and had a most delicious repast. But no sooner had he finished it than he fell into a deep sleep, for the food was all drugged. Here the prince became impatient and fretted at the delay which the dwarf made. But as hours rolled away and the dwarf made no appearance, the prince's brow became clouded at the prospect of certain death which awaited him. Then when it was an hour to sunset, the merchant's daughter said :—"Prince, you are lost. Prepare to meet the reward of your temerity." "No, I have not yet lost my wager. It is an hour still to night and my servant may return in the meantime," said the prince, with the greatest coolness and indifference, though he had but little hope in his heart. Then the prince asked Weak-sight to see what was the matter with the Gootia Deo. Weak-sight looking towards the north cried out :—"Ha, ha, the rascal is sleeping under a tree. Wait, Master, I will soon awake him." Saying this he took up his bow, and discharged a well-aimed arrow at Gootia Deo, and it fell with a loud whirr near the ear of the sleeping dwarf. The sound at once aroused Gootia, who rose up, rubbed his eyes, looked towards the sun and finding it was still one hour to nightfall went up to the lady and with the greatest composure and without betraying his own weakness, asked her to accompany him. Then without giving her any time to reply, he caught her by the waist, put her on his shoulder and placed her before the

Plate XVIII.

Gootia Deo carries the lady through the air.

merchant's daughter just as she was going to order the executioners to cut off the head of the prince. Great was the joy of the prince, his companions and the crowd assembled, at this sudden change of fortune, and at the very hour in which the prince was to have been executed, he was joined by the ties of matrimony to the merchant's daughter.

THE STORY OF THE SEVEN GOLDSMITHS

In a certain city there was a firm of seven goldsmiths, who were very famous for their wonderful workmanship. One day they were called upon by a powerful nobleman, who lived out of the town, to make some ornaments for his wife. The seven friends started forward towards the castle of the chief, and passing through dreary forests reached it safely. The nobleman himself came out to receive them, and conducted them into a large room where everything was ready for their work. The chief was a man of a very sullen and repulsive aspect, and at first the goldsmiths were frightened at his sight and thought him to be a fearful ogre. They would have resigned the work and returned home, but that the nobleman promised most handsome remuneration for their labour and great rewards when the work should be completed. So the greed of the goldsmiths prevailed over their good sense and they stopped in the castle to prepare the jewels and ornaments.

The chief, showing all the arrangements which he had made for their work, such as, the furnace, the blow-pipes, charcoal, &c., led them to another room, which was smaller in dimensions, and in which there was a bedstead and a she-goat. Then the chief said: "This is your sleeping room. That which we left behind is your laboratory. You will retire after your daily work into this room, drink the milk of this goat, and go to sleep on that bed which will accommodate you all. You will get no other food but the milk of that goat, but think not that it will be less nourishing than the most richly cooked dishes. Her milk has the virtue of strengthening the body and sharpening the intellect. She will yield sufficient milk for you all. But mind, you must finish your work within seven days. Now go and begin your work at once."

The goldsmiths did not like much the imperious treatment of the nobleman and much less the accommodation provided for them. However, they began their work and laboured on it all the day, and did a good deal, and hoped to finish it in less than the allotted time. When it was dark, they went out of the laboratory, changed their dress and milching the goat began their supper. They found that the chief had not at all exaggerated the virtues of the animal, for in fact the milk was so very sweet and delicious, that they had never tasted anything equal to it before: and as soon as they drank it they felt a strange exhilaration, and feeling drowsy, they went to sleep. The bed, however, was found to be too small for seven, but it just accommodated six of them. So one of the friends was obliged to sleep on the ground, while the other six slept on the bed.

When it was about midnight the goat began to lick the soles of the feet of the goldsmith who was lying on the ground, and by degrees sucked up the whole life blood of the poor artizan, and the fellow died without any noise. Then there was a clap of thunder and a strange blue illumination in that room, and the nobleman came in and said :—"Sister, art thou happy? Sister, is thy hunger satiated?" The goat replied :—"Brother *Rakshas*, I am happy so long as you keep me so, my hunger is satisfied so long as you give me human blood." And then there was another clap of thunder, and the nobleman and the corpse were both gone out of the room.

Next day when the goldsmiths awoke they found that one of them was missing and they searched him everywhere but could not find him. Then they began their work with great misgivings and the chief reminded them that they must finish it within the stipulated period, of which one day had already passed, and six only were remaining. The friends worked harder than usual, but being one less, could not do so much as they had done the day before, but still they hoped to finish within the time agreed upon. They laboured without a minute's interval of recreation or rest from early morning till late at night, when at last feeling hungry they went to breakfast on the milk of the goat. As soon as they drank it, they again felt the same drowsiness and went to sleep on the bed. But to their surprise they found that the bed had contracted in length and breadth during the day and could not now accommodate more than five persons. So this day also one had to sleep on the ground. The milk possessed mysterious virtues and no sooner had they lain down than they became perfectly unconscious. Again when it was midnight the goat licked the feet of the sleeper on the ground, and sucked up his blood and again the nobleman appeared asking the same questions as before. After which the chief and the corpse vanished.

The next day the friends found that one more of their number was missing, and again they searched everywhere unsuccessfully and returned to their task with hearts frightened at the strange disappearance of their two comrades. They, however, were afraid of leaving off their work

Plate XIX.

The goat sucking up the life-blood of the artizan.

through fear of losing the rich rewards promised, and incurring the anger of the valiant chieftain. But with all their efforts the five could not do so much work as the seven. When at night they went to sleep, the bed was still more contracted and now could contain only four. That night also they lost one of them. Thus they lost one of their comrades daily, till at the end of five days only two remained. Then the two friends said to each other :— "Friend, we will sleep with our *chotis* (locks or tufts of hair in the middle of the head) tied together, so that none may vanish without awakening the other."

The night when they went to sleep, the bed accommodated only one of them, and the other slept on the ground, but with his hair tied to that of his friend on the bed. When it was midnight, the goat again sucked up the blood of the sleeper and the nobleman again appeared and asked : —"Sister, art thou happy ? Is thy hunger appeased ?" The goat replied as before :—"Brother *Rakshas*, I am happy so long as you are happy, my hunger is appeased so long as you give me human blood." So the nobleman vanished in a clap of thunder together with the corpse.

The other goldsmith, who was sleeping on the bed, was aroused out of his sleep as soon as the goat had begun to suck the blood of his comrade, for he felt a pull at his head. Thus he heard and saw all that transpired that night and trembled with horror and fright when he found that the castle belonged to terrible *Rakshases* whose food was the blood and flesh of man.

No sooner was it morn than the goldsmith rose up, and on the excuse of making his morning ablutions went out of the castle, and ran for his life. The goat learned at once of his flight, and immediately changing herself into a beautiful damsel, began to run after him, crying in a very melodious voice :—"Husband dear, husband dear, where are you going away ? Do not leave me behind, take me with you." But the goldsmith knew that it was all a syren's song and that she was a monstrous *Rakshasi*. So he began to flee with greater speed. In the way he saw a large banyan tree sacred to the god Shiva. So he climbed up to its highest branch and, earnestly calling upon the divinity, cried out :—"Protect me, O Shiva, Lord of spirits and ghosts ! Protect me from that terrible R*akshasi*." His prayers were heard, and when the *Rakshas* woman came to the tree and saw the goldsmith on its top, she tried to climb it but could not. Then she sat down under it and went on weeping and crying :—"O cruel husband, why have you abandoned me ? Come down to me. I am afraid of climbing such a tall tree, otherwise I would have come to you. Do descend, O dear lord of my life and solace of my heart." She made many such wails, and wept and sobbed, beating her breast, and pulling her hair, and the noise of her loud lamentation ran through the woods.

By chance a Rajah passed by that place on a hunting expedition and seeing a beautful young lady weeping under the tree went up to her and consoling her, learned the cause of her sorrow. Then looking up to the goldsmith who was perched upon the highest branch, he said :—"Fellow, why do you treat so badly such a good and sweet wife ? Come down and take her home." The poor fellow, afraid of telling the truth, and thinking that even if he did so, no

Plate XX.

"   ee and saw the goldsmith on its top."

one would believe him, replied :—"Your majesty may take her away. I renounce all my claims on her. She is nothing to me." Then the Rajah, happy to get such an easy prize, addressing him said :—"We do not accept gifts from our subjects, but purchase them. Here are two *lakhs* of rupees for her. Come down and take it." "Put it under the tree," said the goldsmith, "I have made a vow not to descend so long as she is within sight." The Rajah, accordingly, put the purses under the tree and taking up the seeming damsel, placed her in a beautiful conveyance and brought her to his kingdom and married her with great pomp and *eclat*.

The Rajah had a favourite horse, a favourite dog and a favourite son, whom he loved very much. The first thing which the *Rakshasi* did was to eat up the horse one night, and throw its bones in the palaces of the other *Ranis* (queens). When the Raja saw next morning that his horse was gone, he came at once to his new Rani, the *Rakshasi*, on whom he doted with strange infatuation, and told her that his horse was nowhere to be found. The wily ogress said :—"Search for it in the palaces of the other Ranis." The Raja repaired to the houses of his other Ranis, who were seven in number, and searched their palaces and found the bones of his favourite horse there. He was, of course, very enraged with his Ranis, and heavily rebuked them for their supposed crime, and in spite of their strong protestations would not believe them to be innocent. However, at last he spared their lives, but kept them in disgrace.

Next day the dog was missing, and the day after his favourite son, and the blame of their disappearance was also laid on the shoulders of the poor Ranis. The Raja was infuriated and ordered them to be beheaded, but on account of the strong intercession of the Prime Minister, and also because the ladies were *enceinte*, the Raja pardoned them their lives but ordered them to be thrown into a dark well without any food.

The poor Ranis lamentitg their misfortunes began to live in the well and to starve. They would have been forced to eat one another to allay the burning fire of their hunger, had not the eldest Rani brought forth a son. Then they unanimously cut the child into seven portions and ate it. Thus they lived for sometime on the flesh of the child. Next the other Rani gave birth to a son, and the babe suffered the same fate as his brother. Thus one after another the six Ranis gave birth to a son, and every one was devoured by the famishing mothers. When the seventh gave birth to a son the others said :—"Now sister, kill it, and let us have its flesh to eat, we are dying of hunger." She replied: "Sisters, I will not kill my son. Here are six pieces of flesh which you gave me, but which I never touched. Eat and have your hunger appeased, but let my son live." Saying which, she brought out the six pieces which had fallen to her share and distributed them amongst the other Ranis. Seeing this the god Shiva was pleased with her, and coming down into the well in the shape of her father, said to her :—" Daughter, I have heard of your misfortunes, but could not find up to this time any opportunity of communicating with you. Henceforth you will get daily eight dishes full of food, one each for you and your sisters and the other one for your child." Having said this he went out of the palace and the Ranis were supplied with food by invisible hands and began to live in that well happier than before.

The virtue of the celestial food was such that within one year the child grew as big and strong as if he were a youth of twenty, and then he one day asked his mother :— "Mother, have I any father, uncle, grandfather, or not? Where are they ?" The Rani wept bitterly and observed :— "Son, you have no father, but you have your *Nana*, that is, my father, who lives somewhere in this city. He is a carpenter, and supplies us with food." The Prince replied :—"Mother, bless me and permit me to leave you, for I will go and search out this relative and see whether I cannot get out of this horrible and dark place." His mother dissuaded him very strongly but he was resolved to go. At last she bade him adieu with tears in her eyes and the Prince went out to search his *Nana* or maternal grandfather.

Following the directions given by her mother, he found out the house of her father and going up to him said :— "*Nana* dear, I have come to you to see you and the wonders of the place." The old man was very much pleased to see his grandchild and asked him what he could do for him. The Prince replied :—"Make for me a wooden horse of such wonderful workmanship that it may fly in the air and gallop on the earth as I should bid it." The carpenter telling his grandchild to stop with him for some days, began to work on the wooden horse. He finished the machine in a week and then presented it to the Prince. Great was the joy of the young man to find such a useful object, and riding on it he went to the palace of the Raja.

Going straight to the palace where the Raja was

holding his Darbar, he offered his services to him. The Raja was soon prepossessed in his favour, though he did not, of course, know him to be his son, and employed him at once as the captain of his guard, and sent him to keep watch over the palace of his new wife, the *Rakshasi*. The Prince going up to the palace rode round and round the building on his wooden horse and frightened all civil persons by his courageous bearing. His arrival soon produced a commotion among the inmates of the palace, so that the cruel ogress herself peeped out of the window to see who this new watch was. As soon as she caught a glimpse of his face, she at once recognised in it the lineaments of the Raja, and new him to be the Prince born in the well.

So when it was night she put off her rich dress and jewels and, wearing a worn-out and dirty cloth and dishevelling her hair, she retired to the hall of anger. When the Raja came to the palace he looked for the Rani, but not finding her in her usual place called the maids of honor and asked them where the queen might be. They replied most humbly:—"The Rani has been weeping all day and beating her breast, and has gone to the hall of anger." The Raja hastened there, fearing that there must have happened something very wrong to have annoyed the Rani so much. When he reached the place, he found her rolling on the ground bedewing the floor with her tears. The Raja falling on his knees entreated her to tell him the cause of her grief, and after much solicitation she replied:—"Do you think I have no heart? Send me at once to my father's. It is long since I have heard anything from them. Send semebody at once to bring the news of their health, and also the singing

Plate XXI.

" Mámá (uncle), Rám Rám (how are you), good day."

water and the *Vanaspati Chauval* (the rice-lord of the forest), a plant which yields cooked rice and grows to the height of forty yards. Procure for me these things soon, or else I leave you. Send this young guard on this expedition, if you love me." The Raja promised most solemnly to do as she directed. Then calling his son he said :—"My brave young man, go at once and bring the singing water, *Vanaspati* rice and news of the queen's relatives. Haste as thou valuest thy life, and return as soon as thou canst. Take this letter from my wife to her father."

The Prince at once rode forth and took the road to the city of the *Rakshases*. He travelled on for months and months till he came to a dense forest, where alighting from his horse he began to travel on foot. When he had travelled long, he came upon a lion in the way, very fierce to behold. The Prince was very much frightened, but, not losing his presence of mind, he stepped boldy towards the lord of the forest and said :—*Mama* (uncle), Ram Ram (how are you), good day." The lion who had thought that there was a nice morsel for him in that young man, was sorely bewildered when he found that the new-comer was his nephew. So he welcomed him mildly :—"Come, nephew, come, go in and pay your reverence to your *Nani* (maternal grandmother], she is there." The Prince went in to the lair and said :—"*Nani*, Ram Ram," and was welcomed by her equally. He tarried there for sometime, and then went forward in his journey. Further on he met a wolf, whose clutches also he got out of by establishing the same close relationship. Thus he crossed that forest full of wild animals by calling every ferocious animal he met with *Nana*, *Nani*.

"cousin," "friend" or other such endearing names. When he emerged out of the wood, he saw a small thatched hut. He entered it and saw a *Yogi* immersed in trance. He stood with joined palms all the while the saint was in contemplation; and as soon as he opened his eyes, the Prince prostrated himself before him and said:—"O great soul, help me in my enterprise. Tell me where I can get the singing water, the *Vanaspati* rice, and the relatives of the queen. Where dwells the person to whom this letter is addressed?" The *Yogi* graciously told the Prince to tarry there that day and he would show him the way to-morrow. The Prince lodged there for the night, and slept on a mat on the ground. When the *Yogi* saw that the traveller slept soundly, he took the letter and breaking the seal, read it by the light of the *Dhuni* (the perpetual fire which burned before him). The contents of the letter were:—

"Dear brother,—As soon as you see the bearer, kill and devour him. Yours affectionately, THE GOAT RAKSHASI."

The *Yogi* burned the letter, and taking up pen, ink and paper wrote the following:—

"Dear Brother,—The bearer of this is my son and your nephew. Treat him kindly and send through him the singing water and *Vanaspati* rice. Yours &c., THE GOAT RAKSHASI."

The *Yogi* then put this letter in the bag which the Prince carried. When it was morn, the holy hermit pointed him out the road to the land of the *Rakshases* and instructed him how to proceed, telling him:—"If you succeed in your enterprise, do not leave behind a single bone which you may find in the castle of the *Rakshases*. Bring them all away."

The prince thanking the holy man for his good advice, bad him good-bye and hastened on his journey. After many difficulties he reached the castle of the *Rakshas*—the same castle occupied by the seeming nobleman who had invited the goldsmiths. On reaching the castle he was led before the chief and presented the letter. On reading the epistle, the *Rakshas* was greatly rejoiced, and embraced him heartily under the mistaken idea that he was his nephew. The chief, who was the king of the ogres, then invited all the ogres and presented the Prince to them, telling them not to molest him in any way. Then he led him to his mother who was a very old and ugly ogress, and consigned the Prince to her care. The Prince began to live in the castle apparently quite contented and happy, but inwardly planning how to encompass his object. He managed to get into the confidence of the ugly ogress, and one day asked her :—"*Nani* (grandmother), show me the wonders of this castle. I wish to know wherein lie your life and death, for, dear *Nani*, I love you and *Mama* (uncle) and all *Rakshases* so much that I am afraid lest anything might injure you." "Do not be afraid on our account," said the hag, "we, the race of *Rakshases*, bear charmed lives. We fear no death. Come with me and I will show you what I mean." She then conducted him into a large hall in which there were innumerable birds kept in cages, parrots, peacocks, pigeons, sparrows, wood-peckers, larks, &c. The collection of birds was grand and unique, and the Prince thought that he was in an aviary. Then the old *Rakhshasi* said :—"Prince, these birds are our lives; as long as these birds live, we live, when they die, we die. You see they are protected with great care and cannot be injured by anybody, and so we also cannot meet with any harm. This black daw is my life, that rook is your *Mama*, my son's life, and this pea-hen is thy mother, the Rani's. The Prince then asked :—"*Nani*, where are the singing water and the *Vanaspati* rice ?" The ogress then conducted him into another room and showed a bottle full of a very clear, limpid liquid, out of which there flowed a most enchanting music. "This," she said "is the singing water." Then taking him to the garden she showed him a very tall tree and said, "that is the tree of *Vanaspati* rice."

The Prince congratulated himself on thus learning these secrets of the dreadful castle. Then he was shown many other halls and rooms, some of them full of gems, diamonds, gold and precious stones. He also saw the room in which were stored the bones of those persons who had been devoured by the *Rakshases*. Then being on the wait one day when the *Rakshases* and the *Rakshasis* had both gone out of the castle to a marriage feast of the ogres, the Prince finding the time very opportune, entered the hall of life and taking hold of one at a time began to kill the birds by pulling out their legs, wings, and wringing their necks. The Prince spared the life of the pea-hen alone. The corpses of the *Rakshasis* and *Rakshases* made a mountain before the castle gate. Then the Prince taking the bottle of the singing water and a branch of the tree of the *Vanaspati* rice, and tying up all the bones of the dead persons eaten by the ogres in a bundle issued out of the castle and came to the hut of the *Yogi*.

The Prince presented the spoils of the *Rakshas* castle to

the hermit. The holy person taking together the bones of all the victims sprinkled the singing water on them, and, behold, they all came back to life; and amogst them were the six goldsmiths. As soon as the goldsmiths saw the *Yogi*, they recognised in him their comrade and great was their happiness. The *Yogi*-goldsmith then related to them how he had escaped from the clutches of the *Rakshases* and how he had performed austerities and devotion for the sake of his friends and the ruin of the cruel *Rakshases.*

Then the *Yogi* also revealed to the Prince the true history of the Rani, saying:—"O Prince, know that you are the son of the Raja on whose service you undertook this dangerous journey. The Rani who has sent you so far is the cause of all the misfortunes which you and your mother and step-mothers have suffered. But now her days are numbered. Let us all accompany you to the Raja's court and expose her." The Prince dismissed all the rest of the company, but taking with him the seven goldsmiths, the singing water, the *Vanaspati* rice, and the pea-hen, entered the forest. He again paid visits to his Uncle Lion, Uncle Wolf, Uncle Tiger, Uncle Cobra, Uncle Elephant and others of the forest. They were much pleased to see him, and everyone of them presented one of their young cubs, &c., to the Prince. The Prince accompanied by this delectable company issued out of the forest. There on the entrance he found his wooden horse, and riding on it he went towords the city followed by the curious train of birds, beasts and other animals. He appeared in this array like a show-man carrying a moving menagerie.

When he came to the out-skirts of the citv he changed

his dress, and assuming the garb of a juggler, he and the seven goldsmiths went to the Darbar and announced that they would perform the wonderful magic-play called the *Rakshas* unveiled. The Raja called together a great assembly to witness the performance. Then the Prince began his show. The spectators raised loud cheers when they saw him moving fearlessly among his strange collection of wild animals. Then he struck the flute, and at once the animals began to dance in a wonderful circle round and round the Prince. He then planted the branch of the *Vanaspati* rice, and it at once grew up into a tall tree, and cooked rice of sweet flavour rained in copious showers before the spectators and all who tasted declared never had they eaten anything equal to it. Then he dug a large tank and threw the bottle of the singing water into it and at once the whole tank was filled and a delightful music filled the whole palace. The performance lasted for seven days, and on the last and seventh day the Prince said :—"Now we are going to show you our last and wonderful show :—The dance of the pea-hen." Then he brought the pea-hen, and ordered her to dance. The bird began to dance and at once the *Rakshasi* Rani came out of the palace and began to dance before the whole assembly. The Raja was horrified at this, but held his peace. Then the Prince broke one leg of the pea-hen, and behold! one leg of the Rani became broken too. But still the pea-hen went on dancing on one leg, and the Rani also danced on one leg. The Prince then pulled out one wing of the bird and the Rani lost one arm, but still the dance went on. At last the Prince broke the neck of the bird, and the Rani uttering a loud scream, and resuming

Plate XXII.

" The dance of the pea-hen."

her original shape of a large forty-yard long *Rakshasi* fell dead on the spot. Then the whole assembly cried out with one voice :—"What is this, whom have we here ?"

Then the Prince stepping forward addressed the assembly:—"Here you see the *Rakshasi* who has been the ruin of this fair kingdom." Then the Prince went out for a short time.

The next scene was still more wonderful. There came out seven goldsmiths, each leading a Rani by the hand, and followed by seven Princes. Addressing the Raja they said:—"Here are the most injured ladies, your Ranis, and here are the seven Princes, your sons. Take them and embrace them." Then the *Yogi* goldsmith related the whole story;—how the Ranis were forced to eat their sons, and how they had been revived by the singing water, and all the adventures of the youngest Prince.

The joy of the Raja and the whole Kingdom knew no bounds. Even the favourite horse, the dog and the Prince were revived.

THE STORY OF HIRA AND LAL.

In a certain city, there lived a poor grass-cutter, who used to eke out a poor livelihood by daily bringing grass from the jungle, and selling it in the city for an anna or two. One day, as usual, he rose early in the morning, and went out of the town to cut grass. When he had cut a sufficient quantity to form a bundle of ten seers or so, behold, he found that he had forgotten behind the rope with which he used to bind it. The grief of the poor grass-cutter might well be imagined, for he was to lose all the labour of the day. As he was in deep despondency, his eye fell on something like a rope glittering in the sun a few paces from him. He went to see what it was, and when he came near it, he found that it was the carcase of a dead snake. So he was very glad to find the dead snake wherewith to bind the grass. So with the utmost eagerness, he picked it up, when lo, it was no more a dead snake, but a sparkling ruby, or Lal, of the greatest value. The poor labourer was at first somewhat astonished, and frightened by this sudden metamorphosis, but soon overcoming the new feeling, he carefully tied the ruby in his *pagri* or turban, and returned home, when it was about dusk. Thinking that such a beautiful thing (for be assured the poor fellow did not know the value of the gem) was fittest for the king, he went next morning to the palace, and presented it to the Raja. The king was very well pleased to get such a precious jewel, and paid him handsomely for it, so that the poor grass-cutter had no more necessity to cut grass for the remainder of his life.

Plate XXIII.

" She began to tend the little baby with the greatest affection."

The king taking the ruby, went into the *zenana* and gave it to her beloved Rani. As soon as the queen took it up to admire its brilliancy, how pleasantly was she surprised when she found that it was no longer a ruby, but a very sweet baby just born ! As the queen had no children of her own, she began to tend the little baby with the greatest care and affection. And since it was a ruby, which was changed into a child, she called it by the name of Lal. As Lal began to grow in age and beauty, he exhibited all the signs of royalty and greatness. When he was of eight years of age, his father sent him to a school in which the princes and the princesses of the realm were taught. In that school there also read a very beautiful princess called Hira (or diamond). Lal and Hira soon became very intimate, and began to love each other, before they were very long together. Years passed and their childish love grew stronger and stronger. At last the king, the father of Lal, heard about it, so he at once ordered him, at the risk of his displeasure, to cut off all connection with Hira. In the meantime Hira, having finished her education, was soon going to be married to a very powerful Raja, who was old, one-eyed and stooped in his gait. When the news of the approaching nuptials of Hira reached Lal, he became almost frantic with grief and disappointment. So one night he stole out of the palace, saddled a very swift horse, and rode to the kingdom of Hira's father. When Lal reached the city, it was the day when the marriage was fixed to be solemnised. The bride Hira came out of the palace accompanied by a long procession of gaily dressed persons, who marched with lights and drums through the well-decorated streets. Lal had posted himself at a conspicuous part of the street, and, as soon as the procession reached the palace, Hira caught sight of him, and was very much pleased and knew her deliverance was nigh. As the marriage procession proceeded, Lal found an opportunity to whisper something in the ear of Hira. When the procession had reached a certain part of the city, and the people were absorbed in witnessing the brilliant illumination and fireworks, or hearing the ravishing odes of the nautch-girls, Hira slipped away unperceived, and joined Lal. At once she put off her female dress, and put on a male dress which Lal had with him, and which was of the same cut and colour as the one which he was wearing. When thus dressed no one could tell that Hira belonged to another sex, so completely did the dress fit her ; and as she was of the same appearance and height, the two seemed like twin brothers. Then Hira and Lal riding on two horses went out of the city and rode with the greatest speed possible. On and on they rode, and the hoofs of the spirited steeds gave out flashes of fire, and the woods began to ring with the clatter of their hoofs: but on and on they rode till the sun went down and the stars appeared in the sky.

When it was dark and they had ridden sufficiently far from the city to elude all pursuit, they took their lodgings in a poor hut by the roadside. There was an old woman living in that hut who bade the travellers welcome. Now the hut belonged to two very powerful robbers, the husband and the son of the old woman, who had not yet returned from their nightly work, and the poor lovers had no idea of the danger to which they were to be exposed. Hira being rather fatigued, laid herself down to rest, and the maid-servant of the old woman began to rub and press her legs and feet to induce sleep. As Hira was half-dozing and half-awake, she felt a drop of water fall on her leg, and on looking up saw that the maid-servant was weeping. Hira asked her the reason of her sorrow, on which the maid-servant wept more and more, and at last whispered out: "The house in which you have taken shelter, belongs to two very cruel robbers; they are out now on robbing, and will soon return and murder you both." On hearing this Hira at once jumped up, went to Lal and told him all about the house. Soon they bade adieu to the treacherous old woman, and riding on their horses, rode forth in the dark. The hag made all efforts and excuses to stop them, now telling them about the darkness of the night, the lateness of the hour, and then enlarging upon the dangers of the road. But the lovers did not listen to her. So when she found that they would not return, she ran after them crying: "Two fat birds are flying away, two fat birds are flying away." Her husband and son, who were just returning from their depredations, heard her cry and understanding the signal, at once gave chase to the fleeing lovers. Lal, seeing that two men were pursuing them, discharged an arrow, which pierced the heart of the robber's son, and he fell down dead. On seeing this the father returned home vowing to wreak vengeance on Lal. In the meantime Lal and Hira reached a *serai* where they stopped for the night. When it was day, they found an old man sitting outside, who offered himself to be their groom. Lal took him under his employment, and when the morning had advanced, they rode forth on their journey accompanied by the groom. When they had reached a lonely spot, the groom suddenly gave Lal a strong blow, and cut off his head. After killing him, he went to Hira, and raised his sword to knock off her head too. But she pleaded very hard for her life, saying that she was not a man as she appeared from her dress, but was a woman, and that she was willing to marry him, if he spared her life. The groom was no other than the dead robber's father, and after some hesitation, he accepted the offer, and both began to return towards the hut. When they had ridden a few minutes, Hira looked up towards the sky, and laughed loudly. This irritated the old robber, who was of a morose temper, and he sharply said: "Close thy teeth thou slut; why art thou laughing so?" But Hira, pointing to the sky said: "Look up, look up, what a beautiful kite!" As soon as the robber turned his face up towards the direction pointed out by her, she drew out her sword, and in the twinkling of an eye cut off the robber's head, and, spitting on it, rode back to the place where was lying her dead lover. When she reached that place, she raised a loud cry of lamentation over the dead body of Lal, and all the passers-by who passed by that road began to pity her. As luck would have it, there passed by that road the divinities, Shiva and Parvati, and seeing Hira weep so piteously, the latter asked Shiva, "Why is this girl weeping?" The god Shiva replied, "*Devi*, if thou want to hear the reasons of every weeping maid, then thy heart would almost be broken by the tales of human misery. *Devi*, forbear to ask any question." But Parvati was moved by Hira's lamentations, and would not stir a step

Plate XXIV.

. cut off the robber's head."

forward till she had forced him to tell her the reason of Hira's grief, and to cure it. On being thus pressed Shiva told her of the death of Lal, and approaching Hira, he took the dismembered pieces of Lal's body and joining the head to the trunk glued them together with the blood taken out of his own divine veins; for the blood of the divinity being *Amrita*, Lal at once revived, and the happiness and gratitude of Hira knew no bounds. She fell flat on the ground before the deities and worshipped them. When she had arisen, the deities had vanished.

Then Hira and Lal, riding on their steeds, went forward. After travelling for many days they reached a very large and populous city, and took their lodgings in an inn, where Lal leaving Hira behind went out to make some purchases. He entered a large street and at every shop made some purchase or other, and, giving the price, told the shopkeepers to keep the thing in their shops as he would take them away on his return. So he went on from one shop to another, and at every shop where he made any purchases advanced the money and went forward. At last he came to the end of the street where there was a betel-seller's shop. He went to the betel-seller, who was a sorceress, and asked for some betels. She said: "Come up, sweet lord, I will give as many as you like." Lal, who did not know her character, went with her, where the wicked sorceress enchanted him into the form of a goat.

Here when Hira saw that he did not return, she went out in search of him. She as usual was dressed in the male attire. When she entered the same street in which Lal had made purchases, and when she passed by the shops, the merchants mistaking her for Lal, offered her the thing purchased by him. She answered she would take them on her return. As she went on, every shop-keeper offered her something or other, and she made the same reply. When she reached the shop of the betel-seller, that wicked sorceress told her nothing. Hira at once made a shrewd guess at the truth, that her Lal was there. So she went to the betel-seller, and asked for some betels. The sorceress replied:—"Come up, sweet lord, I will give you as many as you like." "I am not so foolish as the other," said Hira, and went away. As she was passing by a certain street, she saw that an old woman was cooking some sweetmeats, and was weeping and weeping all the while. Hira went up to her and asked:—"Mother, why are you cooking these sweetmeats, and why are you weeping?" The woman said:—"What do you ask, my child? It is a very sorrowful tale. The king of the city has a daughter to whom every night a human victim is offered. To-day it is the turn of my son to be sacrificed. These sweetmeats are for him and I weep for him." Hira said: "Do not weep, good mother! I will go instead of thy son to the terrible princess. Give me these sweet things to eat my fill." The old woman was but too glad to find such a willing substitute, and gave Hira all the food prepared. When Hira had eaten to her satisfaction, she rose and went to the palace. She was soon conducted by the royal officers to the chamber of the princess. Hira, being in male attire, passed for a young gallant and was treated by the princess with all the show of love and kindness with which she treated her victims. When Hira had taken some refreshment, a priest was ushered in, who joined the two princesses in the nuptial tie. Then Hira and the princess retired to a private chamber. There a sudden change came over the princess who had appeared a moment before so meek and loving. She was foaming at the mouth, tearing her hair, and frightful to behold. Her eyes shot forth burning flashes, and shone like two live coals. She rolled on the ground, and writhed and blasphemed. At last her rage was somewhat slackened, and the princess fell into a deep swoon. While she lay thus insensible, her left thigh burst open, and a terrible black snake of the deadliest species issued out of it. As soon as the creature had completely come out of the thigh it darted towards Hira with a fearful hiss and great fury. Its forked tongue was frightful to behold. But Hira, though frightened, did not lose her presence of mind, and as the reptile approached to bite her she cut off the snake's head with a blow of her sharp-edged sword. Hira remained all the night with the insensible princess and by ministrations brought her to her senses. Soon the news reached the king that the snake, who had possessed his daughter so long, had been killed by a valiant youth, called Hira. The king was mighty well-pleased with this, and calling up Hira asked her what reward she would have. Hira asked in return half an hour's sovereignty over the city. The king gladly laid down his sceptre and crown, and placing Hira on the throne commanded all his officers to obey strictly whatever Hira ordered.

When she ascended the throne, the first thing she did was to send a crier into the city, who loudly proclaimed: "Let it be known to all that the king has ordered all citizens, male or female, young or old, to go before His Majesty with all their cattle, beasts, and birds immediately." All rushed towards the palace, taking with them every living creature which they possessed, and when they assembled before the king, and their names were read out, it appeared that the betel-seller was not amongst them. Officers at once ran to the house of the betel-seller and brought her bound with her goat and laid her before Hira. As soon as the goat saw Hira, it ran towards her and began to frisk and jump around her. Hira knew at once that it was Lal and asked the sorceress to sell it. The sorceress said: "Most puissant king, I have kept this goat for sacrificing to mother *Kali* in the coming new-moon day. It being a religious vow, your majesty's most humble slave cannot sell the goat." Hearing this Hira cried out: "Officers, bind that infernal sorceress, and let her be burned at a slow fire." Soon the officers of justice caught hold of her, and carried her to the place of execution and put her to death. Hira took possession of the goat, and by certain *mantras*, for she knew white magic, restored Lal to his human form, and acknowledged him before the whole assembly as her beloved husband: and putting off her male dress assumed the garb of her sex and went into the *zenana*.

The princess was very much mortified at finding that Hira was no man. But she soon overcame her disappointment, and was married to Lal. Thus Lal began to live there and passed his days pleasantly in the love and company of his two wives.

One day the princess asked Hira: "Dear sister, tell me

Plate XXV.

" Hira took possession of the goat, and restored Lal to his human form."

what is the caste of our beloved husband, Lal, for, though we know that he is the adopted son of a Raja, still some mystery hangs about his birth. As thou art his beloved, so pray ask him this question." Hira said: "What is the use of this knowledge to us? Are we not happy in his love, and are we not basking in the sun-shine of his face? What more do we require?" But the princess would not listen to all this, but insisted upon knowing the caste of her husband, and obliged Hira to promise solemnly that she would question Lal about this. So, Hira going up to Lal, asked him what was his caste. Lal was very much grieved at this, and sorrowfully said: "Dear Hira, do not ask me this; you shall regret having asked it." But Hira was bent upon knowing the truth. So Lal took her to a river, and coming to its edge, he said: "Do you still wish to know my caste?" Hira replied;—"Yes." Then Lal entered the water up to his knees and repeated:—"Are you still determined to know my caste?" Hira said: "Yes, my lord." Then Lal proceeded deeper into the stream till it reached to his neck, and again asked:—"Do you still wish to learn what is my caste? It is not yet too late." But Hira answered as before:—"Yes, I do." Then Lal entered deeper into the water, till his whole body was submerged and only a tuft of the hair of his head remained on the surface to mark the place where he was standing, and he asked from under the water, "Hira, are you still bent upon knowing my caste? Forbear; still there is time, or you will ruin the whole of your life." And the voice of Lal, from under the stream, sounded hollow and strong as if he had already become the denizen of another world.

But Hira's resolution did not waver, and she answered :— "I do." No sooner had the words been uttered then even the tuft of hair disappeared, and behold, in the place where a moment before Lal was seen and heard standing, there floated a large black snake. It remained visible for a few seconds, and then suddenly vanished. Hira waited and waited for the re-appearance of Lal, but no Lal did she see again, and loud and piercing was the cry which she gave forth when she realized the extent of her misfortunes, and wept and cursed for the remainder of her life the folly of her impertinent curiosity.

THE STORY OF RAJA VIKRAM AND THE FAQIR

Vikramaditya, King of Ojain, was one of the most powerful sovereigns who ruled India and was famous for his strict and impartial administration of justice. He often inspected the condition of his people and discovered the real state of affairs by mixing among them, alone and in disguise. In this way he came to know many strange and startling things and unravelled many mysteries. Therefore it was seldom that justice miscarried in his reign.

A *yogi* once entered his dominions and took up his residence on the opposite bank of the river on which the city was situated. There he raised a small thatched hut and lighting a large sacred fire (*dhuni*) in the middle of it, he sat in the very midst of the burning element. Soon the fame of his miraculous power and great austerities spread through the town and many came to see and adore him. A band of disciples and followers soon gathered around him and daily the number of converts to his doctrine began to increase. So much so that even the infection spread into the palace of the Raja; and Vikram had soon reason to suspect that all was not well with this seeming *yogi*, and that some conspiracy against his life was being secretly hatched under this garb. Therefore, to find out the truth he, one night, slipped out of the palace, and putting on a disguise swam across the river and hid himself in a corner of the *yogi*'s hut.

What he saw in the hut sent a thrill of horror into

his heart, and his courage was severely put to the test at the sight which met his view. He found the *yogi* seated in the midst of the fire, and before him lay a ghastly corpse. The dead body lay flat on its back, and a person, in whom the Raja recognised one of his discharged and discontented minister, was sitting on the chest of the dead body. He was repeating some *mantras*, and now and then putting a flower immersed in red sandal paste, with leaves of *bel* and incense, into the mouth of the dead body. The terrible ceremony of raising the corpse was being gone through and after an hour or so the ex-minister exclaimed ;—"Speak, O son, speak." Then Vikram saw to his terror the lips of the dead body move, but heard no sound. Again the ex-minister cried out :—"Speak, O son, speak. Thee, O my beloved son, have I sacrificed to mother Kali, in order to wreak vengeance on the ungrateful Raja. Speak, O son, speak." At the end of this earnest and vehement adjuration, the murderer of his son put a fresh quantity of flowers, sandal paste, *bel* leaves, &c., into the mouth of the corpse, and again the lips moved but without uttering any sound. Again the cruel father and ex-minister cried out for the third time, but without success. The *yogi* seeing the failure said :—"Have patience, my child ; there must be some stranger in this room, who without initiation has penetrated into our mysteries, and, therefore, the sacred and mysterious *Devi* does not vouchsafe a reply." Then raising his voice the *yogi* said :—"Whoever thou art that watchest our sacred and secret proceedings, be turned into a dog." Thrice he repeated this, and Vikram tried to go out of the hut, but he found himself rooted to the spot

Plate XXVI.

The dismissed minister sitting on the chest of his son's corpse.

and at the end of the third repetition, he was instantaneously changed into a dog and began to live in the hut.

When it was morning and the Raja did not return to the palace, great was the fear of the ministers and the other officers of the state. But in order to allay the public excitement, it was given out that the Raja was indisposed and would not hold a Durbar for some days. In the meantime secret messengers were sent in every direction to find out the whereabouts of the Raja, but without success. Then the ministers and the wise councillors of the court consulted together and unanimously resolved to ask the advice of the old astrologer Varahamihir. Going up to him, they requested him to tell by his calculations the fate of their beloved Raja. The astrologer found out by his art the whereabouts of the Raja and the metamorphosis which he had undergone by the curse of the *yogi*. Then addressing the councillors and courtiers Varaha said :—"Sirs, it is very difficult to extricate our monarch from the clutches of this terrible sorcerer. He is a mortal enemy of our Raja and would most gladly have killed him but that he is prevented by the four *Virs* (guardian spirits) who protect Vikram. But though they have saved him so long, soon even their power will be of no avail when the *yogi* shall have completed the horrible ceremony of raising the dead body. In the coming new-moon, the mystic rites will end, and then the four *Virs* must lose their power before the superior power of Kali. Something must be done immediately to save him." Saying this he dismissed them, and long remained absorbed in gloomy contemplation.

Then by slow degrees the face of the astrologer brightened and he summoned his twin sons to his presence. Relating to them the unfortunate condition of the Raja he said :—"Children, we have long eaten the bread of the King; now is the time to show our gratitude. We must save him, though at the peril of our own lives. Are you prepared to embark in this dangerous enterptize ?" The twins, who were two very handsome young lads, replied in one voice :—"Father, when were we not ready to obey your commands and our King ? Tell us how we can be of any service in this emergency." The happy father then took them to the river-side, and showing them the hut which was on the opposite bank, said :—"There you see the cottage of the sorcerer. At the door of the hut you will see a black dog ; that seeming dog is our beloved Raja. I will change you into two deer, and you must go and entice away the dog to this bank. The river is not very deep, and the dog will follow you as soon as he sees you. The influence of the *yogi* extends as far as the middle of the river, and not an inch beyond. So run as quick as you can, and bring the dog out of that limit with the greatest speed. So long as you are on the other side of the middle of this stream, you are within the control of the *yogi* and your life is at his mercy ; on this side of it you are safe." Having given them this caution, the astrologer changed the twins into two very graceful deer that swam through the river towards the cottage of the *yogi*.

The deer reached the door of the hut, and no sooner did the dog perceive them than with a deep growl he ran after them. The deer at once plunged into the water, the black dog chasing them. The howl of the dog roused the

Plate XXVII.

"The kite plucked out one of the eyes of the foremost deer."

yogi from his trance, and he saw that the dog was chasing the deer. At first no suspicion of the real nature of the case entered his mind, but looking intensely at the deer he pierced through the magic coat and found that they were human beings. At once the *yogi* changed himself into a kite, and flew in the air after the deer, with the intention of plucking out their eyes. The four *Virs* guessing his object raised a duststorm in the air and prevented the kite from perceiving his prey. By this time the Raja and the twins had almost reached the middle of the stream, when the kite piercing through the storm came down with great velocity and plucked out one of the eyes of the foremost deer. The next moment the three, the two deer and the dog, had crossed the middle line and were out of the baneful influence of the *yogi*. The kite hovered high in the air but dared not cross the line.

When they reached the opposite bank, the astrologer restored them to human shapes and great was the gratitude of the Raja for this help. The loss of one eye of the younger brother cast a temporary damp on the rejoicing of the party, but still the whole city was full of happiness and joy at the news that the Raja had recovered from his dangerous illness through the help of the astrologer. The adventures of the Raja and the *yogi* were kept strictly secret. But the Raja found that the party of the *yogi* was daily increasing in strength and numbers. The protecting spirits, the *Virs*, also informed him that their influence for good would stop at no distant date, before the malignancy of the *yogi*. The Raja, in this extremity, asked the advice of the astrologer in order to counteract the machinations of the sorcerer.

Varahamihir after calculating for sometime said :—"O Raja, my powers are not sufficient to cope with the *yogi.* I know only three sciences, while he is the master of thirteen sciences. In my trance I have searched throughout this world, but have found no one his superior in learning and magic art, except the daughter of the King of China. She knows fourteen sciences and can save you. If you can marry her, your life is safe." The Raja having heard this, assembled his ministers and giving them the charge of the affairs of state, went out alone with his horse towards the country of China. Though the councillors strongly dissuaded him from this dangerous journey, yet he would not listen to them but went out of the city on his river-horse that moved swift as the air.

He rode on and on for many days and then asked a passer-by—"Friend, whose dominion is this ?" The person addressed looked with amazement at the questioner and said :—"Do you not know this ? All this country belongs to the good and great King Vikramaditya." The Raja rode on and wherever he asked he found that it was his own kingdom. Never had he realised so vividly as now the extent and riches of his dominions, and all the more intense became his desire to preserve it in his dynasty at all hazards, by counteracting the machinations of the *yogi.* After months of riding he crossed his frontier and entered the kingdom of China and it took many weeks more before he reached the capital city. When he arrived at the principal city, it was dark, so he did not think it advisable to enter it at that late hour, and, therefore, he stopped in a garden outside of it. Tying his horse to the trunk of a tree, he stretched himself on the ground near it and being weary, soon fell into a deep sleep.

As fortune would have it, a gang of thieves passed by that way, and seeing the river-horse took it for a good omen, which augured success to their undertakings. The leader of the thieves, therefore, vowed, saying :—"Whatever booty we shall get to-day we will divide amongst ourselves and this auspicious horse." They then entered the city and broke open the royal treasury and robbed it of all its precious stones and jewels, and passed out undetected. Then coming to the tree where Raja Vikram was still soundly sleeping, they sat down and divided the spoil. A precious necklace, called the *nau lakha har* (nine lac necklace) fell to the share of the horse. The thieves, therefore, putting it round the neck of the animal went their way. Soon after their departure, the burglary was discovered, and the officers of state ran in all directions to find out the audacious criminals. Some of them came to the spot where Vikram was sleeping, and seeing the necklace on the horse naturally took the sleeper to be the thief. So rousing him with no gentle hand from his sleep, they hauled him, bound hand and foot, together with the wonderful river-horse, before the Emperor of China. The Raja could have easily explained away the appearances, which were against him, and exculpated himself from the false charge, if he but chose to do so. But he was unwilling to put aside his incognito, and preferred to suffer the punishment of a felon. The Emperor seeing that the charge was fully established against Vikram, ordered the executioner to cut off his hands and feet and throw him thus mutilated into the public square.

There lay Vikram exposed to the taunts and ill-treatment of the people, groaning heavily under the pain which the barbarous punishment had inflicted. Exhausted and faint with the loss of blood, he remained there all the day long, unpitied and uncared for. At last, when it was night, an oilman passed by that way, and seeing him in that sad plight, was moved with compassion at his youth, beauty and misfortunes. Coming up to him he bound up his wounds and carried him as gently as he could to his poor abode. The wife of the oilman was a vicious shrew, and as soon as she saw what her husband had brought, she cried "O you blockhead and fool, what have you done ? Why have you brought this ugly *doond* (cripple) here ? Know you not that he is a criminal and has suffered this fate for his daring villainy ? If it be known that we have sheltered him, the Emperor will surely have us pressed in the mill. Go and leave him where he was." But the kind-hearted oilman would not listen to this heartless advice, and said with greater animation than was his wont :—

"Wife, I have brought this helpless creature with my eyes open to the consequences of the discovery. I have called this youth my son, and you must also consider him as such. No selfish consideration shall ever deter me from doing that which I consider to be right and humane. Go and prepare some balsam to dress the wounds of this poor creature." The woman obeyed him and reluctantly dressed the wounds of Vikram and began to nurse the patient. In course of time, under the kind treatment of the oilman and the grudging one of his wife, Raja Vikram's wounds were healed and he began to regain his strength. When he was perfectly cured, the oilman placed him on the seat of the oil press and he was carried round and round the mill by the oxen. Thus the Raja would sit there all the day and be driven all the time. He was helped with food and drink and in fact everything by the oilman and passed his time sitting on the mill.

One day the oilman seeing that his protege required bathing, as he looked dirty and greasy, said to his wife :—"Dear, wash my son to-day as he does not appear tidy." Raja Vikram interrupted him saying :—"Father ! I would not be washed unless you wash me in the tank which is in the summer garden of the princess." Hearing this the shrew went into hysterics of rage and said :—"Look at this presumptuous *doond*, he would not bathe but in the waters of the princess's tank. Know you not that that tank is for your betters, and that no male footsteps have ever trod the golden pavements of that garden ? O husband, you will never do such a foolish and dangerous thing, as to gratify this most absurd and unreasonable whim of this most ugly *doond.*" The husband mildly replied :—"Certainly I will. You must remember that he is my son, and I must satisfy this simple desire of his, cost what it may." Therefore, when it was dark, he took up the Raja on his shoulders and carried him to the summer garden of the Princess of China. Fortunately for them they found the garden unguarded at that moment and the oilman took him and placed him on the banks of the tank. The Raja then bade him depart and come to take him away after midnight. The honest oilman was at first afraid to leave his helpless adopted son alone, but was persuaded by Vikram to leave him there. The loving creature retired with a heavy heart full of misgivings.

When the oilman was out of sight, the Raja hobbled into the tank where the water was not deep and bathed as best he could. Then coming out of it, he changed his clothes and sat down to *puja* (worship). Having performed the *puja*, which lasted about three hours, he looked towards the sky and saw that it was verging towards midnight. Then he sang out in a deep, full and sonorous voice, a weird, strange and soul-stirring air, the *ragini Dipak*, invented by himself and known only to him. It was this music that had enslaved the invisible races of the air and fire, and made them pliant instruments in his hand, it was this music that was another name for Vikram. As soon as the *Dipak* was sung by the gifted Raja, all the lamps in the city which had gone out were lighted of themselves and the people started up in amazement at seeing their lamps burning which they had extinguished when they had gone to sleep, for such was the virtue of the *ragini Dipak* (the Illuminator). Louder and higher rose the music, and intenser and brighter burned the lights, and as the music fell and died away the lights also sunk in their sockets and were extinguished and the whole city was again immersed in the same darkness as it was in before. The princess also was awakened when the lamps were thus lighted, and witnessed the strange phenomenon, and knew at once that it was the work of no one else but Raja Vikram. How strangely did her heart flutter when she made this discovery, for it was the highest ambition of her soul to see and wed that great monarch of worldwide fame. She knew also that Vikram

Plate XXVIII.

"Then he sang out the *ragini Dipak.*"

had come in disguise, and she found out through her great knowledge of the secret sciences that he was putting up with an oilman. Beyond that she could not learn, and her science was at fault.

Here when it was past midnight, the oilman crept into the garden and carried back the Raja to his humble dwelling and putting him in his bed went to sleep. The sun was up, but the poor oilman fatigued with his night watch was still in his bed when he was roused by the royal officers who came to summon him before the princess. The poor fellow was trembling all over, and was sorely afraid in his mind, since he thought that his trespass into the garden had been detected. When, however, he was brought before the princess, he saw that all the oilmen of the city were already there and were standing with joined hands. This gave him some courage, for whatever might be the occasion of his being called there, surely it had no connection with his nocturnal visit to the garden. When he had taken his place among the oilmen of the city, the princess turning to the officers said :—"Are all the oilmen present? Have none been forgotten or omitted?" The officers bowed assent, and then the princess turning towards the oilmen said:—"Look ye, fellows, by six o'clock to-morrow morning, let each and every one of you supply me with a hundred thousand maunds of oil. If you fail to do so, you and your family will all be pressed out of their lives in the mill," and then she dismissed them. The oilmen returned home weeping and crying and cursing the preposterous humour of the princess.

When our oilman returned from the palace of the Princess of China, he was sad and despondent, and as it is natural under such circumstances he picked up a quarrel with his wife. The vixen, learning the reason of her husband's ill-humour, flew into a rage and said:—"O thou ass, see the results of thy folly. Did I not tell thee not to shelter this evil-omened *doond?* Since he has been here, affairs have gone from bad to worse, and now they have reached the worst stage of all. Whence wilt thou get such a preposterous amount of oil? What wilt thou say in answer to our royal princess to-morrow? O! death is inevitable and it is all owing to thy stupidity." With this she set up loud lamentations and bewailing; and well might she do so; the poor oilman himself did not know how to console her, though he knew that his poor protege was not to blame. That day no fire was lit in his house, and no hearth blazed in hospitable glow, and the whole family remained weeping and mourning without food or drink. The helpless poor Vikram sat on the mill, without food, and when it was evening he called the oilman and asked him what was the matter that no flour was kneaded, no oven was lit up, nor any food cooked. He learned the cause, after much difficulty; for the oilman kept weeping and the vixen went on railing and cursing her husband and his protege. Raja Vikram then said:—"Father, if we must die, as seems so very probable, let us die at least like men. Why should we starve ourselves and meet *Yama* (the good of death) half way. Let him come and take us away sound and healthy. Let us not die with our stomachs empty. Go and have our food prepared." After much reasoning and solicitations of this sort, the poor oilman and his shrew of a wife were prevailed upon to cook their food, and eat and drink, though it was their firm belief that they were eating their last meal. The poor couple oppressed with the sad fate which awaited them in the morning did not get a wink of sleep for a long time, but at last nature overpowered them and their eyes were closed for an hour or so.

As soon as Vikram saw they were asleep, he sang in a low voice the *ragini Bhairabi*, and at once his four guardian spirits (*Virs*) made their appearance, and with joined palms addressed the Raja :—"O you the scion of the family of fire (*agnikula*), how long will you hide your dazzling splendour in this obscurity? How long will you remain in this helpless unknown state? Tell us your will, and we are ready to obey." The Raja said :—"My trusted friends, I shall soon emerge out of this obscurity. But now you must help me again as you have been doing so long. Bring one hundred thousand maunds of the best kind of oil." The *Virs* vanished and in an instant the hut of the oilman and the adjoining street were full of thousands of large black jars containing the oil.

Though the oilman's eyes had closed, he did not get any refreshing sleep. He dreamed horrible dreams, and the last one was so terrible that he jumped out of bed with a fearful cry that roused the whole neighbourhood. He dreamt that the officers of justice had come to fetch him, and were hurrying him bound hand and foot to the place of execution. The delusion was kept up, even when he opened his eyes: for seeing the row of oil-vessels, he imagined them to be soldiers, and thus he kept on crying:—

"O help, help, they have come to murder me." It was after some time, and when he saw that the so-called soldiers did not move that he was convinced that it was all a dream. His sorrow was turned into joy when he saw so many jars of oil, and little did he suspect to whom he was indebted for this kindness. Therefore, with a happy heart he went up to the palace, early in the morning, before any other oilman had arrived, and informed the princess that the oil was ready.

The princess had gained her object, she had come to know for certainty that Raja Vikram was at this oilman's house, for no one else except his famous *Virs* could have procured so much oil at such short notice. So she dismissed the other oilmen who had also come by this time to the palace to inform her of their inability to meet her demand; and then she told our oilman to tarry. When all had gone, she asked him—"Oilman, if thou valuest thy life, tell me truly whom thou dost harbour in thy house." The oilman replied with much hesitation that he had no one living with him, but his wife, and an innocent, poor, helpless creature, the *doond*, whom he had picked up from a public square, and adopted as his son. The princess at once saw in this seeming *doond* the real Vikram, and therefore addressed the oilman thus:—"Look thou! two months hence, on the full moon day, the Emperor, my father, will hold a great Durbar of *swayambara**, to which will come all the Rajas, Princes and the chiefs of the world. Come thou also on that day and, bringing thy *doond* (as

*The choice of a husband by the bride herself.

thou callest him) with thee, stand in some prominent place." With this command she dismissed him.

On his return home, the oilman announced to his wife the approaching *swayambara* of the princess, and then turning to the Raja he said:—"Son, thou art very lucky; thou shalt see the grand ceremony of the selection of a husband by the princess. I will carry thee to the palace, for I have been ordered by the princess to do so." The Raja understood quickly that his retreat had been discovered by the subtle princess and that he would gain his object, for what else could have been her meaning by inviting him, if she had not made up her mind so select him. The two months passed away in great bustle and preparation in the capital of China, and now the day of *swayambara* arrived at last.

Who can describe the rich and gorgeous scenery of that royal assemblage? Kings, Princes, and Rajas thronged from all quarters of the globe and pitched their tents in and around that imperial city. The pavillion in which this galaxy of crowned heads met was as richly decorated as the persons of the guests who had graced it with their presence. All sat expectant and with throbbing hearts, every one thinking himself the fortunate candidate on whom the nuptial garland should fall. In a corner of this vast assemblage and out of the sight of the gazing multitude stood the oilman carrying on his shoulders the mutilated Vikram. He had dressed himself and his protege in his best, and his best was a long way off the worst worn by the meanest menials of the pettiest chief in that company. With the oppressive sensation of being an intruder in this noble assembly, the poor oilman stood rooted in his place, his heart sinking within him.

At last the princess entered the pavillion attended by two of her playmates. She was a blaze of beauty, and burst upon the concourse with overpowering effulgence. All looked with speechless admiration on her graceful form and dazzling splendour. She carried a garland of sweet-smelling flowers in her hand, and cast a hasty glance on the assembly. But she saw not the object of her search in their midst, and then she looked on every side. What can escape the searching glances of love? The oilman, though hidden in a corner, was detected by the princess and she at once went there with firm and unhesitating steps, and to the wonder of those proud and mighty guests, she put the garland round the neck of the *doond.* The Emperor of China felt himself greatly humiliated, and the guests were exasperated, at this seemingly absurd choice.

But according to the laws that govern the *swayambara* the election was made and there was no means of getting out of it. The Emperor of China was forced to give his consent to this marriage, and calling up the oilman told him to bring the bridegroom with proper pomp and procession on the next day. Knowing that the oilman was too poor to defray the expenses of such a marriage and to arrange everything for the same, he appointed his prime minister and his treasurer to manage it all.

The oilman returned home, carrying on his shoulders the bridegroom elect, and announced the happy news to his wife. Then he set about making hasty preparations for the coming marriage, but Raja Vikram peremptorily prevented

Plate XXIX.

"She put the garland round the neck of the *doond*."

him from doing anything out of the way. He said :—"Dear father, why should we trouble ourselves with these hasty preparations ; they are perfectly useless. Do not stir at all." The oilman wondered very much at this strange request but nevertheless complied with it. The officers of the king who came to manage everything were also driven away by the proud Raja Vikram. When it was night, Vikram told his adoptive father to carry him once more to the private garden of the princess. The oilman reluctantly did as asked.

When Vikram was put on the edge of the tank, he dismissed the oilman, saying :—"Father, go away now but come to take me before dawn." The oilman went out of the garden, but his curiosity being aroused, he returned to it by another passage and hid himselfin a corner to witness the doings of his protege.

Raja Vikram after finishing his ablutions as before, sang out the *Dipaka ragini*, and no sooner did the oilman hear it than he stood rooted to the spot with ecstasy. Again as the strange and weird notes floated far and wide on the waves of air, the lamps burst forth into light, and again the princess awoke and saw the mysterious phenomenon. But this time she did not remain idle ; so changing her shape into that of a heavenly chorister (Apsara) she flew on golden wings of magic out of her palace and went to the garden whence the music proceeded. She saw there Raja Vikram, as she had expected, but the Raja did not recognise her in her new shape. Then the seeming Apsara, coming up to Vikram, saluted him and said :—"O great Raja, I have been pleased with your song, so ask any boon." The Raja humbly said :—"O thou Dweller of the heavenly mansions of Indra, make perfect my mutilated limbs." As soon as the seeming Apsara heard this request of the Raja, she vanished and returned immediately with the cut off pieces. Then she joined then to the body, and behold the Raja was whole again. The Apsara then vanished and returned to her palace.

Then the Raja invoked his four *Virs* and lo! they appeared in all their glory and might. "What commands Your Majesty?" said they. "Behold we are ready." Then the Raja said:—"Friends of life! whom I have won after long years of austerities and *tapas*, ye have always served me faithfully and diligently. Now hastens the period of your emancipation, for soon shall ye be released from human thraldom. But be not ungrateful to the man who gave you intelligence when you were unintelligent, who gave you consciousness when you were aimless wanderers of the air without a motive and an object. Now hasten ye, to the four quarters of the globe, and bring together here all my army; let tents be pitched for miles all around the city, let horses and elephants in thousands well equipped and in gold and silver trappings be ready at my command, let the hut in which I am living be changed into a royal edifice, containing treasuries full of precious jewels and gold, and servants in gorgeous livery. In short, do everything befitting Vikram, the Emperor of India: and all this before morn." The guardian spirits with low salutation indicative of unquestioning obedience soon melted into the air.

The poor oilman, who had witnessed all these strange things from his hiding place, now came forward trembling and prostrated himself before the Raja, saying :—"Forgive me, O mighty monarch." The Raja at once raised him from the ground and addressing him kindly said :—"Father, think of me always as your son. I can never repay the kindness which you showed me when I was in adversity. Henceforth you will always be a father to me and share with me command and the kingdom. But let us now hasten home, as the dawn is already appearing in the East."

Then quickly going out of the garden they returned home. The oilman was astonished to find that what he had left a hut only a few hours ago was an imperial palace now; and his shrew, dressed like a queen, came out to receive them. Wonderful was the change which good fortune and the knowledge of the august position of their protege had wrought in her temper. While she was all curses and scoldings before, she was now all bows and adulation.

In the meantime, the sun had arisen and the obedient spirits had fulfilled their commands. The news soon reached the Emperor of China that a mighty army had surrounded the city during the night. To whom they belonged and with what object they had come was still a mystery. The Emperor at once hastened out of his palace, bareheaded, barefooted, with a straw in his mouth, in token of subjugation and with the object of propitiating the new invader. The Raja came out to receive his father-in-law and soon dispelled the alarm of the monarch. Who can describe the happiness of the Emperor when he found that the seeming *doond* whom her daughter had selected was the glorious Raja Vikram ? When the news spread throughout the city, all the Rajas and chiefs, who had the day before gone away in great disgust and had planned to kill the *doond*, now returned with great humility and threw themselves at the feet of their successful rival—the great Vikram.

The marriage ceremony was performed with great pomp and *eclat*, and in the evening a great performance of dancing girls was given to the assembled Rajas and chiefs in the large pavillion erected by the *Virs*. The Raja and the princess sat on a raised *dais*, and the others were seated below. While the dance was going on, the news was brought that a band of jagglers, who could perform wonderful feats of magic, were waiting outside to show their talents before that noble assembly. The Raja ordered them to be brought in: and no sooner had they entered than the Raja at once recognised in the headmen of the group, the *Yogi*, his mortal enemy, and the descontented minister. The Raja at once turned pale and the Princess finding out the cause whispered:—"Fear nothing, see how their own malice re-act upon them and kill them."

The jugglers, being ordered to proceed with their play, began it with the performance called the raising of the dead. The ex-minister brought out from a chest the preserved body of his son and stretching it on the ground sat on its chest. The *Yogi* burned fire all round and sat in its midst. Then the other jugglers began to beat drums and tambourines, and the corpse and the ex-minister rose into the air and soon vanished out of sight. Soon there was heard high up in the air the clash of arms and the noise of a fight. Then there fell on the ground now an arm, then a leg, then the trunk and so on till the whole body was complete.

Then the ex-minister also came down and said :—"Rajas and chiefs, here you see the mutilated body of the corpse. I will now make it whole and revive it." He then joined the various parts together, and the *Yogi* gave him some ashes from his *dhuni*, and no sooner was it strewn on the dead body than it was whole and alive, and standing up cried out :—" Father I am hungry, give me food." The ex-minister replied :—" Be thou a tiger and eat our enemy," pointing towards Vikram.

At once the resuscitated corpse was changed into a tiger and sprang towards the Raja. But the Princess waved her hand and the tiger jumped back with a tremendous roar, as if struck by invisible lightning, and, furious with rage and before the *Yogi* could intervene, the angry beast attacked the ex-minister and tearing him to pieces ran out of the pavillion. The *Yogi* seeing the fate of his companion, came out of the fiery circle, and was running away when the Princess again waved her hand, and he stood transfixed to the spot. Then in a voice of thunder addressing him she said :—" Miscreant sorcerer, who hast used the divine powers of thy soul to the basest of all purposes, I cannot punish thee more than what thy own works have ordained for thee. Wander thou henceforth in the world, soulless and senseless, like the beasts of the forests and the birds of the air." Then she waved her hand, and the sorcerer went out—an idiot, devoid of the light of reason, as if the lamp of the intellect had been extinguished for ever by that potent motion of her hand. And Vikram returned to his kingdom with his bride, to the joy of his subjects, and lived happy ever afterwards.

THE STORY OF PRINCE MAHBUB

There was in ancient times a very powerful King of Persia called Mansur-i-Alam (the conqueror of the universe). He was blessed with everything which a man could desire, and had vast treasure and large armies. His subjects were happy and contented under his just and good administration. All praised his great wisdom and noble virtues. But unfortunately he had no son to inherit his enormous riches and extensive domains. One day the king assembled all the astrologers of his realm and asked them to tell him on what particular day, hour and minute, one should be born in order to be a great and powerful king. The astrologers made their calculations and replied :—"Sire ! the child born at midnight on Sunday last will be very fortunate and happy and will be endowed with every royal virtue. So if Your Majesty is desirous of adopting an heir, adopt the child born on that day and that particular hour."

The king hearing this told his prime minister to find out in whose house a son was born at the time mentioned. Messengers ransacked the whole kingdom and brought the news that no male child was born at that particular time, except that the wife of a butcher had given birth to a son. The King calling the butcher asked him to give him his son. The butcher, who was a poor man, gladly promised, saying :—"Your Majesty is the lord of our lives and limbs. You have to command and we to obey." The generous monarch replied :—"Friend, I do not ask as a king but as a private individual. Do you agree to part with your son out of perfect free will and good intention? For I will not otherwise accept the gift." The butcher replied :—"Sire, I offer you my son with the most perfect good-will and without any compulsion. It is my great good fortune that my son should be adopted in such a royal family." The child was then brought and all the ceremonies of adoption were gone through.

When the butcher's son, now called Prince Qassab, grew up, the king appointed wise and learned teachers, by whom great pains were taken for his education. When he attained majority, the king made him viceroy of one of the richest provinces of his empire. Here when in power, the Prince displayed all the evil propensities of his disposition. For though born under auspicious signs, and brought up under good teachers, the hereditary qualities of a butcher, which were ingrained in his nature, manifested themselves in full force. He tyrannised over his subjects and spread terror throughout the country by his atrocities. Reports of his misgovernment and complaints of the persons ruined by his tyranny or disgraced by his debaucheries daily reached the just king, but he did not, out of his good nature, give much credence to them.

In the meantime, the queen who was supposed to be barren, exhibited signs of maternity, and great was the rejoicing of the king at this discovery. He had despaired of having any issue of his own, but was most pleasantly disappointed. He at once despatched messengers to Prince Qassab with the following news :—"Rejoice, O son, for I soon hope to have an addition to our family. Your mother, the Queen, is *enceinte*, and the astrologers have predicted that a son will be born to me. O happy news for you that you will get a brother!" As soon as Prince Qassab got the news, he said to himself:—"Now my evil star has appeared on the horizon. When a prince of the royal blood is born, who will care for a butcher's son though raised so high? Surely my fall would begin with the rise of my brother. Oh, it is painful to lose such a position and rank as I now enjoy. Had I remained the son of a butcher I should have been contented with my lot, but having tasted the fruits of power and royalty it would be very painful to lay them aside. I must go to the city of my adoptive father and see whether I cannot retain my power." Thus musing, the Prince riding on a swift horse went in all haste towards the capital. He reached the palace of the king when it was about midnight and getting admission, for everybody knew him and nobody apprehended the evil purpose which had brought him in such an unseasonable hour to the palace, he at once repaired to the apartment of the king. He found him asleep, and with one blow of his sharp sabre cut off his head. He then went with the bloody sabre in search of the Queen, but she had heard of the arrival of the Prince and had disappeared by a secret door out of the palace, with some faithful attendants. They carried her on swift horses, during the night, far away from the capital, till they, at last, reached a forest, where the Queen dismissed them saying:—"Go now my faithful adherents! and let me remain in this dreary place. If I die of starvation or be killed by some wild animal, I shall have, at least, this satisfaction that I am not murdered by the butcher's son. Leave

Plate XXX.

"Art thou some angel, *Peri*, goddess, or spirit ?"

me now to my fate and go." The poor servants returned home weeping.

The Queen sat there bewailing her hard destiny, when a *zemindar* (a rich farmer) passed by that way, and seeing her was struck with her extraordinary beauty and majestic air. Coming up to her, he said :—"Art thou some angel, *Peri*, goddess, or spirit ? Who art thou ?" The Queen replied :—"I am no angel, *Peri*, goddess, or spirit, but a poor daughter of man, in distress. I was the Queen of this country, and am now a homeless wanderer." As soon as the honest farmer came to know the august rank of the lady, he fell on the ground and kissing the dust said :—"Mother, I am a *Jagirdar* of your husband and all these fields and villages which you see around are yours. Come and live with us ; we are humble, honest people, and you will find comfort if not elegance in our simpler modes of living. Remain with us, and as I am childless, the child of your womb shall I adopt as my own and bring him up with all due care and diligence." The Queen consented and was taken by the *zemindar* to his house, where she remained in disguise as the cousin of the *zemindar*.

In due course she gave birth to a son whose beauty illumined the whole house, and the news spread throughout the village that the *zemindar's* cousin had given birth to an angel. The Queen called him by the name of Mahbub-i-Alam (the beloved of the universe.) When Prince Mahbub grew up, he was sent to the village school, where he read with other boys, sons of the Jats (a caste of cultivators). There he soon surpassed his school mates in learning and physical exploits. While the sons of the Jats took pleasure in playing with bat and ball, the prince evinced his royal blood by playing at archery. He made a rude bow and rude arrows and would shoot all the time in every direction. Though nobody taught him the art, he soon became a very good archer, and could hit the mark from a long distance.

Once the usurper, the brother of Prince Mahbub, held a great tournament in which all the great archers of the kingdom were asked to attend. There were four prizes for the successful archer. First, a purse of five hundred *mohars;* second, a suit of dress out of the royal wardrobe which the winner might select ; third, any horse from the royal stable ; and fourth, a suit of armour and arms, weapons, &c., from the arsenal. The news of the great tournament reached even that secluded village and Prince Mahbub hearing of it set out for the city without informing his mother. The poor Queen thought that her son must have gone to school, but the Prince instead of going there had started for the town. Night came and still the Prince did not return ; men were sent in all directions to search for him, but to no purpose. The Queen sat disconsolate and weeping, and would not take any food or drink, till her Mahbub should return.

The Prince, on the other hand, in company with other archers reached the city and lodged with them in a *serai* (inn). He soon made friends with them all, and asked them to permit him also to try at the mark in the coming tournament. His gentle appearance and amiable temper prepossessed the archers in his favour and they gladly enlisted his name among the members of the company.

The next day was fixed for the tournament, and the archers and the prince went to the place early in the day. There was a large concourse of spectators, and in a rich and splendid pavillion and on a gorgeous throne sat the usurper to witness the performance. At a signal from him the archers entered the lists and one after another shot at the mark. Some came very near to it, others nearer but none pierced the exact centre. Prince Mahbub, who was the youngest of all the lot, now shot his arrow last and it pierced the very centre of the mark. At once there rose deafening cheers and applause, and the whole assembly praised the wonderful feat of the young boy.

The King gave him a purse of gold containing five hundred *mohars* and ordered his vazir to take him to the royal wardrobe, armoury and stable to select the various articles. The vazir conducted him to the wardrobe and the Prince without any hesitation selected the identical suit of dress which was worn by his father, the late King. And let no one wonder at it, for he was guided in this matter by his royal and innate instincts. Accoutred in the dress of his father he went to the armoury and selected those very weapons which the late King used when going out on chase or war, and then entering the stable rode on the very horse which was the favourite of his father. Thus equipped he came before the assembly, and the whole people with one voice, and as if involuntarily, cried out:—"Behold our favourite and just King come to Life." So exact was the resemblance between the Prince and his father, that the people mistook him for the late sovereign. The acclamation of the people disconcerted the usurper, and he was mortally enraged, and yelling out to his servants, said:—"Seize that silly boy and hang him." The servants ran here and there, and raised a great confusion, for in fact they were not at all anxious to obey the cruel mandate, and gave Mahbub every opportunity to escape out of the bustle.

When the Prince came out of the city, he assembled all the archers, and throwing down the purse of gold amongst them rode with all haste towards the village. He returned there after full forty-eight hours and found his mother sitting at the door weeping and crying, "Mahbub, Mahbub." As soon as she saw him, she burst forth into a pleasant laugh, and then wept again bitterly. Then the Prince jumping down from his horse, asked her:—"Mother, what is the meaning of your behaviour? Why did you laugh and weep in the same breath?" The Queen replied with a sigh:—"I laughed when I saw you return in this equipment, which belonged to your father. I wept at the thought of the change of fortune which has brought us to this pass. Now you know the secret of your birth, and the reason of my weeping and laughing."

The Prince hearing this replied with deep emotion:—"Mother, I had some faint glimmerings of this since I had been to the tournament and the people exclaimed that I was just like the late King. But your account has confirmed my doubt: mother! we must not stay a second more in this country. Not that I am afraid of anything from the cruelty of the murderer of my father, but I swear not to eat or drink the food or water of this land so long as I do not wreak vengeance on the accursed head of the usurper. The very air of the country is poison so long as I do not breathe it as a king and avenger of the wrongs of my sire. Mother! arise, let us be off."

When the *zemindar* heard of the determination of the Prince, he was sorely afflicted and entreated him with tears and sobs to change his mind. But Mahbub was firm as a rock, and would not be prevailed upon, though he, too, was equally grieved to part from the honest *zemindar* and his family. However, bidding them a hasty adieu, the Prince and the Queen went their way, trusting to Providence to guide them out of the kingdom.

They travelled on and on without food or drink till they had left behind the kingdom of the usurper. Afflicted with many days' hunger and thirst, and fatigued from their long journey, they now began to search for a hospitable roof where to beg some bread and water, and rest their weary limbs. But the outlook was very gloomy, the place where they had come was a mountainous district that showed no signs of human habitation, far or near. However, after much search, they saw a humble musjid at the foot of the hill. They dragged themselves exhausted and almost lifeless into the house of prayer and saw an old *faqir* lying on a tattered and worn out mattress. The Prince then humbly besought the *faqir* to give them some food and drink as they were dying of hunger. The old man pointing to a niche said:—"Young man, there is a bit of bread in that hole, take it out and eat you both." The Prince going to the place, found there a small slice of cold and mouldy bread not enough to make one mouthful. Then taking it to his mother and presenting the slice to her he said :—"Mother, eat this and support your strength. It is not sufficient for us both, but you stand in greater need of sustenance than my young and vigorous frame. Eat it, mother." But the Queen would not take it, saying :—"Son, I am old and have enjoyed the pleasures and suffered the pains of this transitory life ; I am prepared to meet death. Let me die, as it will make no difference. But live thou, and do thy great work." The Prince paid no heed to all this but went on pressing the bread on her. She refusing and he insisting, they squabbled on for a long time. The *faqir* seeing this observed :—"Travellers, why do you fight for nothing? You both eat this slice, and you will not be able to finish it." Then mother and son ate of the bread, but still the slice remained the same as before, and was not diminished even by an inch. They were fully satiated and the bread was the same as before. Never had they found anything so delicious as this crusty and mouldy piece of bread. Then the *faqir* pointing to another niche, said, "there is the water." The Prince approaching it saw a small earthen jar of water. The contents of the vessel were not sufficient even for a single person, and there was altercation between them as to who should drink, and again the *faqir* said :—"Children of the road, drink you both in the name of the great Allah." And they both drank out of the vessel, and were fully satisfied, and yet the water in it was not diminished by a drop. Then the *faqir* asked them :—"Whence are you coming and whither will you go? You cannot go beyond this mountain; for on the other side of it is a tempestuous and fathomless sea. No ships have ever ventured to sail in its turbulent waters. Return home."

But the Prince replied:—"O holy *faqir*, we have vowed not to return to the land of our birth. The polished mirror of your pure heart has already received the reflection of our sad history on it. We need not say who we are. Help us now in our journey, O holy saint, for nothing is impossible for the divine austerities of your prayers." The *faqir* replied:—"True, O traveller, prayers are accepted by Allah when they rise from pure hearts. What can a sinful creature like me do? However in my travels I have discovered some of the properties of natural objects. I will see whether I can help you."

Then telling them to remain in the musjid and await his return, the *faqir* went out into an adjacent forest. After a short time he returned with two pieces of wood, freshly cut from the branches of some trees, peculiar to those parts. With one piece, he made a short stick about a cubit in length and with the other a torch. Then addressing them, he said: "Here are the things that will carry you across the dangerous forests and vast seas. This torch when lighted will frighten away all fierce animals of the wood or the deep. And this rod, a cubit long, is your ship. Wherever you may put it in the sea, the water of that place, however deep, will at once become fordable, and will never rise higher than the top of this stick. The waters before or behind or around you may be thousands of fathoms deep, but within a radius of fourteen yards from the place where you will hold this stick, the water will never rise higher than a cubit." Then lighting the torch the *faqir* showed them the way over the mountains and conducted them to the sea. There he bade them adieu and returned to his cottage.

The Prince taking the rod in his hand, jumped into the water and placed the rod over the surface of the sea. At once the waters became calm for a radius of fourteen yards, and all of the uniform depth of a cubit, though beyond the magic circle the sea was fathomless and very turbulent. The Queen carrying the torch followed behind and waded through that sea, the water never rising higher than their knees. They saw also the unrevealed wonders of the sea-bottom, such as corals, pearls, sea-flowers and trees. Inexpressible were the delight and admiration of the Prince at seeing these beautiful things, and whenever a new animal or natural object came within the range of his vision, he would cry out most joyously to his mother and running up to it would take it up and show it to her. Thus they went on admiring the wonders of the deep and praising the wisdom of the Almighty. When they had reached almost the middle of the sea, the Prince saw a current of water flowing from a certain direction, and carrying in its flow innumerable rubies of the purest and brightest water. Mahbub, who had never seen rubies, cried out in an ecstacy of boyish joy :—"Mother, mother, behold how beautiful are these pebbles. Of what a glorious red colour they are! O mother, let me pick up a few of them to play with." The mother, who knew the value of these precious stones, the least of which would fetch a lac of rupees or so, was afraid to touch them. She feared that so many valuable and extraordinary rubies in such a strange place boded no good. It must be some temptation of Satan to cause their ruin. So, she strongly dissuaded him, saying :—"Why child, you are the best of all precious stones or pebbles; your love has

Plate XXXI.

Prince Mahbub and his mother crossing the sea.

brought me to this pass; love not these, lest they bring greater misfortunes." The Prince desisted for a while, but he was strongly tempted to disobey his mother's commands, which he had never done before, for the glowing colours of the rubies constantly appealed to his fancy. At last unable to resist the impulse, he secreted one of the biggest of these stones in his pocket unperceived by the Queen. Sometimes good comes out of evil, and this act of disobedience of the Prince, though entailing many difficulties on him, led at last to unexpected results.

The Prince and the Queen, with the help of the *faqir's* rod and torch, succeeded in crossing that vast sea without any serious trouble. They at last landed on the coast of the kingdom of India. Having rested for a while, they proceeded to the capital town of the country, which was situated not far from the coast. They halted at a *serai* outside the city, and the Queen giving some copper coins to the Prince asked him to fetch some eatables from the Bazar. The Prince took the money and went to the shop of a sweet-meat-seller, and fearing lest the Queen should come to know that he had secreted the ruby, thought it better not to keep it on his person; therefore, he gave it to the shop-keeper, saying:—"Brother, give some sweetmeats in lieu of this." The shop-keeper, seeing the stone, examined it closely and finding that it was a ruby of the purest and best kind, could not help admiring it. So weighing out five *seers* of sweet-meats he bound it in one corner of the cloth given by the Prince, and in the other corner he bound five *seers* of *mohars* of the purest gold and gave it to the Prince. Mahbub returned to the *serai* with the heavy load of sweetmeats and gold and put them all before the Queen. Her astonishment might well be imagined than described, when she saw so much gold, and fearing lest he might have obtained them by unlawful means cried out in great anxiety :—"Son, whence have you got so much gold and sweetmeats? I gave you only five copper coins; so if you have done anything wrong, go at once and restore all this money to the person wronged, for good never comes of evil." Mahbub then falling on his knees implored pardon of his mother, saying :—"Yes mother, I have done wrong, but not what you fear. It is not against any inhabitant of this country but against you, most dear and kind mother. In disobedience to your command I picked up one of the red pebbles which we saw in the middle of the sea and all this is in exchange of that." At first the Queen angry with the Prince for this, but then finding that he had been deceived by the sweetmeat-seller she went to his shop accompanied by the Prince. Finding him in the shop, the Queen said :—"Brother, if my son was blind, were you also blind? If he was ignorant of the value of the precious stone, did not you know that it was a *nau-lakhahar*, a ruby worth nine lacs of rupees? How could you deceive a simple boy like this?"

The sweetmeat-seller finding that he had done wrong in thus taking advantage of the ignorance of the boy and being ashamed of his conduct, for to give him his due, he was on the whole the most honest of all the shop-keepers, now implored mercy of the Queen, saying :—" Mother, forgive me my oversight. Look at these coffers and iron chests, you see them full of gold *mohars*. Take them all away;

they will be about seven or eight lacs, and let me retain the ruby." The Queen seeing that it was not a bad offer, consented to the bargain, took the money and went back to the *serai*.

Here the sweetmeat-selller sold the ruby to the vazir at a large profit and the latter in his turn sold it to the king at a large profit. The king taking the ruby went into the inner apartment, and gave it to his only and beloved daughter *Gulrukh*. She wore it round her neck and with great elation of spirits ordered a carriage to be made ready and went out to her garden to enjoy the scene and her happiness in silence. She paced here and there with great joy, and after a long ramble, sat down in a mango grove. On the top of a tree there were sitting a pair of birds, a parrot and a *myna*. The *myna* said to the parrot:—"Friend parrot, relate some interesting story to beguile our time." The parrot replied:—" Ah lady, I fear my speech will enrage you, for I have some hard truths to utter." "Be sure, I shall not be angry with you," answered the lady bird; " go on with your story." "Oh lady, strange are the freaks, the whims of your sex. Once there was a princess, very beautiful and good-natured. Her father one day presented her with a ruby of the costliest kind. The princess who had never possessed such a precious stone was filled with pride and vanity. She wore it and went about showing it to every person. But the vain princess did not know that it did not suit her, that a single ruby was not as good as many; that to wear it, one required a dress befitting it, for without such concomitants it appeared that she was not the rightful owner of the gem. But, however, the foolish princess wearing it, paraded it among all, and never knew her error."

The princess heard all this talk of the birds, and understanding that it was addressed to her, hastened at once towards the palace, rushing to her rooms, threw aside the ruby, and closed the doors and refused to eat or drink, but wept all the time. The king hearing of the sudden grief of his daughter, went to her and entreated her much, saying:—"What ails you, my child, that you are lying down so disconsolate and sad? Has anybody said anything to you, or has anyone looked at you with improper eyes? Are you angry with anybody or has anyone offended you? Tell me what is the cause of your sorrow?" The princess after much entreaty replied with sobs and sighs:—"Father, no one has offended me or cast an improper look on me. I am the most miserable princess on earth. Why did you give me this ruby that has brought down on me the ridicule even of the birds of the air? It does not singly befit me. To be worthy to wear it, I must have a dress befitting it, and a dozen more such gems. Let me know what kind of dress they wear who have got such stones. Get me such stones and dresses." The king promising to fulfil her desire went out.

At once he sent for the vazir and asked him whence he had procured the ruby. The vazir pointed out the shopkeeper, who was asked to find out the travellers from whom he had got the ruby, within twenty-four hours or it would not be well for him. The poor sweetmeat-seller went with a throbbing heart to the *serai* but found no trace of the mother and son there; then he searched the whole city; and

Plate XXXII.

"What ails you, my child?"

when he did not succeed, he went out and began to search in the suburbs. At last, cast down with despair he was returning sorrowfully homewards when he remembered that he had omitted to enquire at a certain new palace which was said to have been built by some unknown merchant in a very pleasant and romantic spot outside the town and on the sea-coast. He at once ran towards the palace, and as he was about to ask the door-keepers to whom such a grand building belonged, whom should he behold but the Prince Mahbub issuing out of it on a beautiful steed followed by a company of riders gallantly dressed and going out to hunt? The shop-keeper who had seen him in another and worse plight was struck dumb at all this grandeur and splendour. He with a deep bow addressed the Prince :—"My Lord, His Majesty the King has called your honour." The Prince, stopping a moment, haughtily replied :—"Go and tell your King, I am not his servant nor his subject that I should obey his summons. If he has got any business with me, I am always to be found at home. He can see me here."

The shop-keeper returned to the king and informed him that the seller of the ruby would not come, but had asked His Majesty to go there. The king, though enraged at this message, however, thought it expedient to go himself to Prince Mahbub. For the Princess *Gulrukh* was breaking her heart for more rubies, and a dress befitting such jewels and it was no time for anger. The king, therefore, himself went to the Prince of Persia and was received with great honour by the latter. They were introduced to each other, and the King of India now learned that the host also belonged to a royal family. The King of India after the usual salutation and greeting opened his message thus :—"Prince, I have come to trouble you for some more such rubies as you sold once to a shop-keeper. Have you got any more ?"

"Thousands," was the ready answer ; "how many hundreds does Your Majesty require ?"

The King was aghast at this reply. All the wealth of his kingdom, and a most wealthy empire it was, could hardly purchase ten such stones, and here was a young man in exile from his own kingdom, possessed of thousands of such costly rubies. Surely he must have got hold of the hidden treasures of Qarun, thought the King, for never had he heard of any king or emperor possessed of so much riches. So with great humility, the King replied :—"Prince, I have neither the inclination nor the means to buy so many, I want only half a dozen such stones, as well as a suit of dress worn by those who adorn themselves with them."

The Prince replied :—"Your Majesty shall have these rubies as well as the dress on the fourth day from this. I must pay a visit to my treasury. Rest assured that you will get them on that day." The King returned full of wonder and amazement at the interview, and anxious to know the hidden sources of such riches.

Here Mahbub taking leave of the Queen, and telling all his attendants that he was going on a private business from which he would return within four days, started alone on his journey, taking of course, with him the magic rod and torch. On a lonely part of the sea-coast where no one could observe him, he lighted the torch and entered the sea. Carrying the light in one hand, and the rod in the other, Mahbub walked through the waters rapidly, unhesitatingly and boldly as if he was a creature of the sea. He dashed through the sea, without stopping to observe the many wonders which met him on every side, and never stood even for a moment to take breath till he reached the middle of the sea and found the current that carried the rubies. He was going to pick up some, when a sudden thought occurrred to him :—"Whence are these rubies?" Eager to investigate and clear up the mystery, the Prince began to trace the current to its source. The higher he went, the more wonders did he see, and found that the stream was becoming narrower and narrower, though he could not measure its depth, for the magic rod kept it everywhere at the uniform depth of a cubit. On and on he went and now the current which was a mile in breadth before dwindled down to a small streamlet a few yards broad. But there was instead, as if to compensate for the loss of width, an inexpressible and delightful odour issuing out of these waters. Never had the Prince smelt such scents in his life; it appeared as if thousands of maunds of *attar* were floating on the waters and spreading a delicious perfume all round. Exhilarated with the balmy air, Mahbub waded through the stream and at last found that it had its origin in a whirlpool, the waters of which were foaming, boiling and bubbling and were circling round and round with tremendous velocity, and making a deafening noise, as if thousands of water-giants were struggling underneath and were fighting for dominion over the deep.

Out of this whirlpool there rose in a column many yards high a spout whose waters were calm and of the purest white and made a strong contrast with the black and boiling waters of the main stream from which it arose. It was laden with rubies and emitted a strong sweet smell and appeared as if some huge monster underneath was spirting it up with immense force which carried it up to such a height. At every gush thousands of rubies were thrown up along the spout, which after dancing in it for a while, fell into the current beneath. The Prince watched this display of whirlpool, spout and gems with absorbed admiration and awe. His courage wavered only for a minute, but his faith in the wand was like adamant. Shaking off all doubts he jumped into the raging pool.

Down and down he went, through the hole, the waters parting above and below him, and becoming perfectly calm and tranquil. For many minutes he fell through the chimney of the whirlpool, till at last his feet touched the solid ground. He saw before him a huge gateway of massive iron, on the northern side of the cave, and a stream of water flowing out of a drain beneath it, carrying rubies and precious perfume along with it. Mahbub seeing that the entrance was closed, entered through the hole of the drain, which was sufficiently large for the passage of a human body, into the interior.

No sooner had he effected his entrance, than he found himself in a strange and wonderful region. He looked back for the gate, but found no traces of it anywhere. He was in a garden of wonderful trees and birds, and saw before him a large palace. He entered it boldly and saw beautiful rooms and halls tastefully and elegantly decorated, but silent and lifeless. He passed from one room to another admiring the grandeur of the scene, and the wealth of the owner of such riches. At last he came to a room which was illumined by twelve waxen and perfumed candles, and from the roof of which, suspended by a chain of steel, hung a human head freshly severed from the body. The twelve candles were placed in a circle round a basin of water placed just underneath the head. Large drops of blood fell drip, drip, drip, into the basin and as every drop fell into the water, it splashed up to a tremendous height and fell in a nice curve into a drain, beneath. As it fell every drop became a beautiful ruby and flowed out of the drain. The Prince stood long looking at the wonderful scene of the transformation of the blood into rubies. How long he remained in that reverie cannot be said, but at length he was roused from it by the sound of some approaching footsteps of some dozen persons or so. The Prince hearing the noise hid himself in a corner in order to observe better what passed in that subterranean hall of mystery.

Mahbub saw from his place of concealment twelve *Peris* of the most elegant shape enter the room. One of them took down the head, another brought from a hidden recess the body. They placed the two parts of the body on a golden bed, and joining the head to the trunk, the twelve *Peris* took up the twelve burning candles, and began to move round and round the bed in mystic circles, singing a sweet but sad song all the while. By degrees their movements round the bed became more and more rapid till the velocity became so great that the Prince could distinguish no forms, but saw a circle of light round the bed. Now the Prince saw that round the circle in which the *Peris* were moving there was flowing a small ring of water of such a strong and overpowering sweet smell that the Prince became almost faint. The perfume which he had smelt in the sea was nothing in comparison with the richness of the odour which this circle of water emitted. Then the dance ceased and the Prince saw that the *Peris* were profusely perspiring owing to the exertions of the dance and the ring of water was formed by the odorous perspiration of these children of the air. This ring of water also joined the drain into which the water of the basin fell, and thus carried out of this mysterious palace precious stones and delicious scent, one the produce of human blood, the other the perspiration of *Peris*.

The *Peris* then stooped over the bed, and every one kissed the face of the dead man and cried out in deep wails: —"How long, O Lord, how long! Nights and days, nights and days for the last fourteen years, have we waited and waited. O when will the sun of hope arise on the darkness of our despair! Arise, O King, arise, how long will you remain in this deathlike trance?" Thus they moaned and lamented, but in vain.

Suddenly there arose sounds of sweet and joyous music, and the Prince and the *Peris* were all startled at this strange interruption. The music pealed louder and louder and the *Peris* recognising the voices of the heavenly choristers trembled with joy, hope and suspense, while the Prince stood enchanted by the ravishing strains that fell on his ears. Then the floor of the room burst open, and out there-

Plate XXXIII.

The Prince doing obeisance to Kwajah Khizr.

of rose the venerable form of the *faqir* whom the Prince had met in the Musjid by the mountain in the kingdom of Persia. He was now clad in garments of light. The *Peris* all prostrated themselves before him, crying: "Khwaja Khizr, Khwajah Khizr, is the hour come?"

The Khwajah Khizr, for such in fact was the seeming *faqir*, said in a deep voice:—"Yes, the time is come and no more shall ye weep." Then turning to the corner where Mahbub lay concealed, he said:—"Prince, come out." The Prince instantly emerged out of his place of concealment and prostrated himself at the feet of the great and immortal saint Khwajah Khizr.

The holy and all-knowing seer, then said as follows:— "Prince, you see before you the corpse of your father. As soon as he was murdered by Qussab, the *Peris* brought his remains to this subterranean palace, the cemetery of the kings of Persia. Know that your ancestors belonged to a race of beings called the *Magi* and commanded the *Peris* and the genii by their wisdom. No son of theirs ever died but his remains were buried in this place by the faithful races that inhabit the fire and the air. But the body of your royal sire was not buried, since no one had performed the funeral rites. Now that destiny has brought you here, perform the said ceremonies to lay at rest his hovering spirit."

The Prince hearing this sorrowful speech, shed bitter tears, and approaching the dead body prayed fervently to Allah for the soul of the murdered King. But as soon as he had done praying, and laid his hands on the body of his father, behold! there burst forth another peal of music from invisible sources, and to his extreme joy and wonder, the head was joined to the body, and the King of Persia sat up restored to life on the bed by the touch of his son. Oh, who can now describe the happiness of the *Peris*? Khawjah Khizr then introduced the father to the son and there was great rejoicing in the land of the *Peris*. Then the holy saint vanished by the same way he had come, and the genii and the *Peris* transported the King and the Prince to the palace of the latter in the kingdom of India. The meeting between the King of Persia and his Queen was full of tears and tenderness and might better be imagined than described.

Here when four days were over, the King of India again came to the palace of Mahbub for the rubies. What was his fear and astonishment when he saw that large strange-looking creatures with horns on their heads guarded the gate, and it was with great difficulty that he got admission. He was conducted to the Durbar room where the Prince and the King Mansur-Alim were seated, and as soon as Mahbub saw him he greeted him with great cordiality, and said:—"Your Majesty, I have not forgotten my promise. Allow me to thank you for the happy result which resulted from your commands. As for the rubies, you will get as many as you require." He then ordered a servant in attendance to bring a cup of water, and then taking a sharp needle pierced his finger, and let fall ten or twelve drops of blood into the water and they all sparkled forth as rubies. The King of India was bewildered at this, but the Prince quickly replied:—"Let it be known to Your Majesty that every drop of blood that flows in the veins of the princes and kings of Persia is more

Plate XXXIV.

The usurper's blood changing into toads.

precious than hundreds of rubies and every tear which they shed more costly than thousands of pearls. I learned this secret from my father, the King." The King of India as soon as he knew that he was in the presence of the powerful King of Persia threw himself on his knees and acknowledged himself his vassal.

The rest of the story is very soon told. The princess of India got the rubies and the fairy dress, and the parrot and the *myna* praised her this time and advised her to marry the Prince who had taken so much trouble to satisfy her whims. As this advice was agreeable to her inclinations and to the policy of the great kings, nothing stood in the way of their connection. A large army was soon fitted out by the King of India, and another by the *Peris* and the genii and they proceeded towards Persia. The usurper Qassab, whose tyranny had alienated all hearts, as soon as he heard of the approach of the invading armies, rallied some mercenary followers and was killed after an ineffectual resistance. His head and body were carried by the *Peris* to the Subterranean Hall, the cemetery of the kings of Persia, and hung up in the same place where the former corpse was suspended. Every drop of blood which fell from the head of the usurper became a deadly ugly toad and floated into the sea scattering poison and putrid odour many a mile around.